PLAYING LEFT WING

From rink rat to student radical

PLAYING LEFT WING
From rink rat to student radical

By Yves Engler

RED Publishing
and Fernwood Publishing

EDITING Gary Engler
COVER DESIGN Working Design
PRINTED AND BOUND IN CANADA BY Transcontinental Printing

A CO-PUBLICATION OF
RED Publishing
2736 Cambridge Street
Vancouver, B.C. V5K 1L7
and
Fernwood Publishing
Site 2A, Box 5, 32 Oceanvista Lane
Black Point, Nova Scotia B0J 1B0
and 324 Clare Avenue
Winnipeg, Manitoba R3L 1S3
www.fernwoodbooks.ca

Fernwood Publishing Company Limited gratefully acknowledges the financial
support of the Department of Canadian Heritage, the Nova Scotia Department
of Tourism and Culture and the Canada Council for the Arts for our publishing
program.

Canadian Cataloguing in Publication Data
Engler, Yves, 1979-
Playing left wing : from rink rat to student radical / Yves Engler.
Co-published by RED Publishing.
Includes bibliographical references.
ISBN 1-55266-169-5
1. Engler, Yves, 1979- 2. Students—Canada—Political activity. 3. Student
movements—Canada. 4. College students—Canada—Biography. I. Title.
LB3610.E55 2005   378.1'981'092   C2005-902607-3

To Trevor Linden, who was my favorite Vancouver Canucks' player when I was growing up. Not only was he great on the ice, carrying the Canucks to Game 7 of the Stanley Cup finals against the New York Rangers, but he always took an active role in the NHL Players' Association.

TABLE OF CONTENTS

CHAPTER ONE

MY YEAR AS STUDENT COUNCIL VICE-PRESIDENT
(AN OLD CHINESE CURSE: MAY YOU LIVE IN INTERESTING TIMES)

There I was, one day a left winger scrapping and scoring for the Chilliwack Chiefs of the B.C. Junior Hockey League, then what seemed like a very short time later, the arena no longer had ice, but the games were just as intense, the battles just as hard-fought.

Instead of trying to dig out the puck from the corner, I found myself crushed at the front of a crowd trying to prevent an accused war criminal from speaking on our campus. Instead of getting a two-minute penalty for obstruction, I found myself with a one-semester suspension for "vexatious conduct" and "stickering" on campus, then a five-year expulsion for attending the student council to which I was elected. Instead of talking to reporters from local papers about my fight with another team's goon, I was interviewed about Concordia University's ban on free speech. Instead of referees I had to deal with campus security guards and the Montreal city police. Instead of hockey, I was playing politics.

● ● ● THE PROTEST ABOUT former Israeli Prime Minister Benjamin Netanyahu's visit to Concordia University kicked off the semester under a new left wing student council and executive. We took office in June and our slate followed in the footsteps of previous left wing Concordia Student Unions (CSU). During their

This warrant, dated September 9, 2002, permits the immediate arrest of Benjamin Netanyahu

terms they had set up a free vegan cafeteria, "The People's Potato", successfully challenged the commercialization of campus space and sent many into a state of uproar with a pro-Palestinian and anti-capitalist student handbook titled Uprising. We'd spent the summer preparing a new (less contentious) handbook and learning our job. While things were busy, they were quiet. We knew things would heat up once the Fall semester began, but no one guessed how incredibly hot the atmosphere would get in our very own version of global warming.

As CSU vice-president responsible for media, one of six paid elected positions, it was my job to get our message out, but I was only vaguely aware of this "warrant" for arrest that appeared on Concordia campus and in downtown Montreal a day or two before Netanyahu's arrival:

WARRANT for the arrest of BENJAMIN NETANYAHU, former Prime Minister of Israel; on the charges of crimes against humanity and crimes of war.

This warrant, dated September 9, 2002, permits the immediate arrest of Benjamin Netanyahu, former Prime Minister of Israel, on the charges of crimes against humanity and crimes of war.

According to verified sources, Mr. Netanyahu will be in Montreal on September 9, 2002, and will be in the vicinity of the Hall Building at Concordia University between 10am to 3pm.

Mr. Netanyahu is to be arrested on sight by either competent authorities or ordinary citizens and residents.

Canada's own war crimes legislation authorizes the arrest and trial of war criminals for offenses committed outside the country. As Prime Minister of Israel between 1996-99, and as an official of the Israeli government, Mr. Netanyahu is alleged to have committed — or to have been directly complicit in — gross abuses of human rights in the Palestinian occupied territories and the state of Israel. These crimes are tantamount to crimes against humanity and crimes of war, under widely recognized and internationally accepted definitions of both the Government of Canada, as well as the United Nations.

Mr. Netanyahu's alleged crimes include:

• Authorizing extra-judicial executions throughout his term as Prime Minister.

• Authorizing the torture of over approximately 2,500 Palestinians in Israeli jails, leading to the deaths of several detainees and injury to many more. The International Convention against Torture — ratified by the state of Israel — as well as the Convention on Civil and Political Rights explicitly prohibit torture under any circumstances.

• Authorizing over 249 house demolitions in the occupied territories — unequivocally prohibited by the 4th Geneva Convention — constituting a war crime in the form of collective punishment.

• Authorizing the construction of 6,500 settlement-housing units in the occupied territories — in contravention of several United Nations Security Council resolutions as well as Article 49 of the 4th Geneva Convention — and increasing the number of illegal settlers in the Palestinian occupied territories by 9%.

• Authorizing the deadly and disproportionate use of force in September 1996 against unarmed demonstrators protesting his order to blast a tunnel under Al-Haram Al-Sharif (Temple Mount).

All of the above-cited crimes are documented and verifiable, by both eyewitness and expert testimony.

Upon arrest, Mr. Netanyahu is entitled to competent legal counsel and due process. He is also entitled to a fair and impartial trial.

Legal authorities in Canada — the federal and provincial governments and their respective law enforcement agencies — are bound to uphold this warrant by virtue of federal statutes. Failure to do so constitutes gross neglect of duty and is criminally punishable.

Those who obstruct or impede the arrest of Mr. Netanyahu, or the

implementation of this warrant, are guilty of "aiding and abetting"
which is a criminal offense.

This warrant is issued in the genuine interest of ending the crimes of
occupation in the Palestinian territories and the state of Israel, in a
spirit of solidarity with the courageous resistance and intifada of the
Palestinian people, and with the aim of achieving a just peace between
the peoples of the Middle East.

One of the many ironies of the Netanyahu incident at Concordia was that none of what transpired on our part was planned. In fact, I'd argue that the whole thing was a series of stumbles. The first of these occurred when the pro-Israel student club Hillel asked the student union executive for permission to use the biggest hall on the downtown campus for the upcoming Netanyahu lecture. The CSU had booked the space for the entire orientation week and so Hillel had no option but to come to us with their request. It was our first contentious issue. In an effort to be fair we voted unanimously to give up the room for the noon-hour meeting. The only dissent came from the orientation coordinator who happened to be Jewish; she argued, "This is going to wreck the whole orientation week."

Right up until the day of September 9th, I didn't know what was going to happen — in the frenzy of orientation week organizing by opponents of the visit went largely unnoticed. As far as I knew people would gather to protest and that would be that. There had been some leaflets, a story in the university paper and some mention of a protest in the mainstream media, certainly nothing out of the ordinary that would foreshadow the events to come.

The night before the protest, I saw police setting up a metal detector on the main floor of the Hall Building (CSU offices are on the sixth floor). Another taste of what was to come came shortly after when I was yelled at by anti-Netanhayu protest organizers for agreeing to give Hillel use of the hall. Only then did I sense the possibility that something significant was about to take place.

⚜ ⚜ ⚜ THE NEXT DAY is a glorious September morning, one of the last hot days of summer. Setting off for school, I get there at 10:00 a.m. and can't help but notice there are snipers on the library roof as well as riot police setting themselves up on Rue de Maisonneuve, which runs in front of the Hall Building where the Netanyahu meeting is supposed to take place.

The side street adjacent to the main building is abuzz with energy and discussion so I hang out, engaging in a few of the lively, sometimes heated, but mostly friendly debates that Netanyahu's visit has sparked. Forty-five minutes later, as more protesters arrive, someone shouts out, "to the other side" and about 50 of us march swiftly towards the sole entrance to the Netanyahu talk on the other side of the building. We arrive to find about a hundred or so people milling about, some waiting in line to get into the talk. We keep moving, right to the front of the line and I end up at the very tip of the pincer movement near the door — kind of like finding yourself in the opponent's corner battling for the puck against a six-foot-five defenceman.

For the first time that day the atmosphere changes to one of confusion and confrontation. We chant slogans and the pro-Netanyahu crowd shouts back. The crush of bodies and the jostling that takes place means I am now in a position, with several other protestors, of effectively blocking the entrance. My only comparable experience was a mosh pit at a Hole concert years ago at the famous old Commodore Ballroom in downtown Vancouver. It is a tight spot, uncomfortable, scary even, as we got locked between the swell of a growing crowd and a barricade of steel and police.

My shorthair clean-cut hockey-player
look had saved the day

Anger is now visible and very audible as those people blocked from entering the talk target us. I can't move and the temperature of the confrontation continues to rise. Then suddenly some huge security guards pull me out of the crowd, forcing me in the direction of police waiting a short distance away. I am immediately handcuffed. Warning signals race through my brain — this is definitely not going to look good — a CSU executive member arrested! The first thing that pops into my head is to tell the cop that "I just lost my ticket" and amazingly he immediately releases me back into the crowd. My shorthair, clean-cut, hockey-player look had saved the day! Had I looked Arab would he have released me?

The scene at the entrance continues to be one of mass confusion, but most people determined to enter the building to hear Netanyahu speak find their way in. Not wanting to tempt fate I head back to other side of the building. I spend a few minutes trying to calm down — my adrenalin is pumping like the Quebec Peewee Tournament semi-final when my Montreal team went into double overtime against the hometown squad. My girlfriend and I then enter the Hall Building through the back entrance. Since classes are taking place on the upper floors students are still being allowed in.

Outside, the crowd of protestors has swollen to four or five hundred, now outnumbering the Netanyahu supporters. A sit-down protest blocks all possible automobile entrances. In a pivotal move, a group of about 50 to 100 protestors branches off from the main demonstration. On entering the Hall Building they discover that barricades block most of the mezzanine and the escalators leading to the main floor. On closer inspection, it turns out that these "barricades" are on wheels and without security guards to back them up. In a quick move, a few barricades are pushed aside, allowing some of the protestors to take control of both escalators (to and from) the main floor. A second area under the complete control of protestors is the "high ground" on the mezzanine, where a balcony overlooks those entering the building to attend the lecture. Inside protestors, whose numbers have swollen to about 200, begin chanting. Everyone who enters the building to attend the talk must walk 150 feet or so past protestors chanting anti-Netanyahu slogans from above. For a while I am one of those people on the mezzanine. In contrast to later media reports, nothing is thrown and I hear no anti-Semitic comments or chants.

Within minutes of the mezzanine occupation, about 15 riot cops appear beneath us on the main floor, blocking the stairs. I continue to participate in the demonstration for about fifteen minutes, then some students trying to attend classes, who are nervous about their safety, request that I talk to a security guard. Based on their concerns I do a quick survey of the whole scene, both inside and out of the Hall Building and things are pretty bad. The welfare of students and staff seems, at best, an afterthought to the security guards and police on campus. I decide that the most useful thing I can do is to go to my 6th floor office to write a quick leaflet about what is unfolding at our school, while the events are fresh in my mind.

Just as I finish writing the few hundred words and start printing I hear booming sounds from below and catch the first unmistakable whiffs of teargas. The scene that follows is one of panic and confusion. Protestors and students on the lower floors scramble to higher floors, while students attending classes head in the opposite direction to escape from the fumes. But no one can get out of the building because the police have blocked all exits. I organize about a hundred students and lead them in the direction of the CSU offices, where we are able to open some large windows to access breathable air. After about fifteen minutes of mayhem, the police finally allow people out through the Mackay Street side exit and Netanhayu's talk is cancelled.

Disoriented and upset, especially about the tear gas, I make my way to the front of the building, where about a thousand protestors face four or five hundred people who had waited in vain to see Netanyahu. At one point a line of riot cops is forced to separate the two groups — that's what I am told — as I am preoccupied with distributing leaflets printed amidst teargas and confusion. Forty-five minutes later, the protest winds down, but an anxious crowd of reporters and camera operators remains. As the CSU media rep I make myself available to them before finally finding time to meet my friend Mike, who is visiting from Vancouver.

Hungry and tired — he from traveling and me from one amazing day — Mike and I head off to eat. Looking up from a za'atar, I see my face staring back at me from the television set. What have we gotten ourselves into? That night there are meetings to strategize about our media response, but everything we talk about is rendered irrelevant, as a short time later Rector Frederick Lowy announces a university moratorium on the discussion of the Palestine-Israel issue. The next day we hold a press conference where at least a dozen media outlets show up to find out what has happened at Concordia on the fourth day of the new school year.

● ● ● THE NEXT MONTH is a whirlwind of activity, as the world appears to converge on Concordia. Television cameras are everywhere almost all the time. Reporters from media outlets across North America, Europe and Israel call day and night. As CSU media vice-president I experience a real life crash course in crisis management. It is exhilarating and exhausting.

● ● ● ON OCTOBER 16, 2002, we decide to set up an information table about the Free Trade Area of the Americas (FTAA). The table is part of the Concordia Student Union's education and mobilization campaign in the lead-up to the October 31, 2002, international student day of action against the FTAA — activities approved by Concordia students through a referendum earlier in the month. On that fateful afternoon two CSU employees set up shop in the mezzanine of ConU's main building, an activity which, according to Concordia's post-Netanyahu regulations (nine days after the protest the Board of Governors [BoG] decided to expand the ban that the Rector previously announced) is dangerous, inflammatory and therefore verboten. The right to conduct student affairs in the two busiest areas on campus has been taken from us. The mezzanine space, however, is supposed to be returned to students as of that morning's BoG meeting.

When the table is set up we are told that the BoG people have backed off their commitment to return the space, but we don't care. Enough is enough. We never accepted the legitimacy of the BoG's decision (with administrative backing) to take away this space from students and clubs.

Shortly after the table is set up, I am accosted by the "Don" — Donald Boisvert, Concordia Dean of Students. He asks me to whom the table belongs. Since the CSU executive is spearheading the campaign and I am the lone executive member present, I "fess up" and take responsibility for this terrifying outbreak of democracy.

I assume the position. With my legs at a right angle to the floor, back straight, numerous flyers strung out across the table and my lungs full of enough oxygen to vociferously denounce the FTAA to passing students, I go to work. In response, Con U security guards decide the situation requires serious backup and soon thereafter the Montreal police arrive. Looking somewhat uncomfortable as they survey the situation — one measly table with a few hundred flyers and a lonely ex-Chilliwack Chiefs Junior A left-winger, current CSU vice-president, they nonetheless ask me to leave since, they insist, I am trespassing. This strikes me as funny. My presence in the busiest spot on the campus where I pay fees, study and am an elected employee of the duly certified student union is being defined as "trespassing" — a concept peculiar to a feudally derived, capitalist notion of property rights that the poor police officers are sworn to uphold on pain of joining the unemployment lines. Nevertheless, with dozens of supporters watching and reporters on their way, the police pass on the arrest option demanded by the Con U security horde.

Three hours later, when all the leaflets have been distributed, the table is removed and I head upstairs to CSU offices to study for a mid-term exam. About 15 minutes afterwards, coincidently once the reporters and most supporters have left (with the exception of one French CBC television crew, who luckily stayed outside in their van, and are able to catch footage of what follows), security chooses once again to confront me.

The ConU security horde busts into the CSU communications office where I am copying notes. (The fact I was doing so the night before an exam later becomes public knowledge, sharply reducing the effectiveness of playing the sympathy card with my professor after I bomb the test.) The security horde demands I leave the building, but I decline their offer. As a student and elected CSU representative, it's my democratic right to be in the student council offices.

Two minutes later a few Montreal police officers knock on the door and, after an exchange of pleasantries, politely ask me to leave. Again, I pass on the offer. They read me my rights, handcuff me and then escort me out of the building to nineteen awaiting

The police graciously help me into their cruiser and question me briefly

police vans and a paddy wagon! Nineteen. Do they know about my reputation as a tough guy from junior hockey? Or had they heard my nickname in peewee (where I played on a line with Canadiens star Mike Ribeiro for one season in Montreal) was Le Train de Vancouver.

On the way out a handful of supporters follow us (ConU security horde, police and yours truly) chanting, "shame, shame, shame." The police graciously help me into their cruiser and question me briefly. I am told not to hang out with such a bad crowd and am released with the warning that Concordia security will charge me criminally if I return to campus within the next 24 hours.

There is one big problem with this request: that exam the next afternoon. (Not to mention the complete absurdity of arresting me after I had already removed the "trespassing table" which was only a problem because security decided to make it one.)

Immediately after being released, about ten of us gather and decide that we can't allow this situation to go unchallenged. An urgent action is needed, so those who are still allowed by the security horde to step foot on campus go about preparing for a protest the following afternoon. The campus is plastered with pictures of the previous night's arrest. A hundred or so students show up for a short outdoor protest, which increases by another hundred when the protest moves inside for some free food. The theme of the protest is "help Yves Engler attend his exam" and some placards are adorned with the slogan "Lowy [Concordia's Rector] out! Yves in!" Later, dozens of people accompany me to my exam. Too bad a few of the better students couldn't have helped me write it — my excuse for a poor mark is a lack of sleep due to all the excitement.

The entire experience is surreal, unlike anything that has happened to me since my hockey days. It's like having a great game when I seem able to skate around or through every opposing player. But instead of hearing a thousand fans cheering, I have become the focus of attention all across Canada. My arrest makes national TV newscasts that night and the story appears the following day in both national newspapers. I get phone calls from parents of my friends back in Vancouver. I get phone calls from my parents. I get phone calls from people I have never heard of before. It's like I am famous simply because I have stood up and said "I have the right to voice my opinion and the university can't stop me." Such a fuss for something that I had always thought was a basic democratic right.

● ● ● ON NOV. 1, 2002, 11 of us are told we face internal university charges over the anti-Netanyahu protest. (A few people —not me — also face criminal charges.) I am accused of being present on the mezzanine on Sept. 9, of "vexatious" conduct, of handing out leaflets on Oct. 16, and putting up stickers on university property. In other words, I am charged with being a student activist. Sanctions sought include expulsion from the university.

● ● ● AFTER MY ARREST (no charges were laid) for the anti-FTAA table the continued ban on discussion of Israel-Palestine issues attracts wide attention with almost unanimous media condemnation of the university's restrictions on free speech. Even the editorial board of the Montreal Gazette, normally no friend, takes our side. The ConU administration has succeeded in turning us into the proud defenders of free speech. We invite two members of Canada's Parliament to challenge the ban, but the administration goes to court to prevent them speaking on campus. The scorn heaped on the university finally becomes too much and less than a week later the ban is lifted.

● ● ● THE POSITIVE MEDIA attention we receive from our free speech fight soon ends, however. The day after the moratorium on Israel-Palestine discussion is lifted Hillel has a table on the Hall Building mezzanine where they distribute anti-Muslim, anti-Palestinian pamphlets and a recruiting brochure for the Israel Defence Forces. The uproar (which was obviously calculated) is immediate. An offended student files an internal charge against the Hillel club, under the university code of conduct. A couple of days later a motion comes to student council asking that Hillel's budget be frozen and its club privileges suspended until they apologize. I and two other executive members speak (we don't have a vote) against the motion, but it passes (only eight of 28 councilors are present) and the media onslaught, which had quieted somewhat, resumes. Again, I have to deal with media from around the world. Again, the CSU becomes the target of editorials from across Canada. We face wild accusations of dictatorial behavior and anti-Semitism.

● ● ● LATE IN JANUARY the hearings for our university charges begin. I am found guilty of vexatious conduct during the Sept. 9 protest and placing stickers for the anti-FTAA rally. My penalty is to be a one semester suspension and a $500 fine. An appeal is immediately launched, but most interesting, the day after my "conviction" is announced, two of the three student tribunal members who have found me guilty attend a press conference where they announce that a member of the administration coerced them into making the decision.

● ● ● EVEN WHEN WE aren't trying to be political events seem to have a way of attracting attention and making life "interesting" — to say the least. In March, the annual Art Matters exhibit organized by Fine Arts students includes an artist's representation of George Bush wearing a cowboy hat with the Twin Towers protruding, penis like, from his pants. The banner dominates the same mezzanine space that protestors had occupied Sept. 9th. Many, mostly supporters of the upcoming war in Iraq, are not amused and yet again, I am dealing with reporters from across North America. The campus has become the flashpoint of differing views. Once again Concordia is synonymous with left-wing student activism.

● ● ● THE TRUTH IS I never planned for any of the events that took over my life that year. The truth is, a few short years before I was playing junior hockey and was not involved in any way with politics. The question is how did I get from there to here?

CHAPTER TWO

THE ROUTE FROM HOCKEY TO STUDENT ACTIVISM

Okay, I admit it: For the first nineteen years of my life I was a jock. A hockey player! Even worse: I was a "rugged left winger" who stood toe to toe with opposing players, slugging it out to the delight of fans cheering on yet another hockey fight.

I'm not going to apologize, or justify, but simply try to explain how I traveled from a universe where skating ability, hand-eye coordination, size, toughness, low body fat, aerobic fitness, anaerobic fitness and mental focus were valued above all else to a milieu where the best things you can say about someone are "she's really committed" or "he's got a good point."

My parents tell me I listened to entire Vancouver Canucks games on the radio when I was four years old, that I carried a plastic hockey stick and "played" along with the action described on CKNW. One of my earliest memories is Chris Quan and I shooting a plastic puck against the next door neighbor's garage and she scolding Chris in Cantonese, even though, as a third generation Canadian he did not speak the language.

I began playing organized hockey when I was five, a week before my first day of kindergarten, during which four of us were locked into a closet by a new teacher who had suffered a nervous

Not only did I play the game I was fixated on knowing everything about the sport

breakdown. The lesson learned: Hockey is fun, school is not.

I played for Hastings and then Burnaby Minor Hockey where my teammates and friends were kids with last names such as Leung, Rosen, Zacarelli, Vitaljic, Bains and Tsoukalas. Most of my teammates had parents who were born in other countries, many of whom spoke limited English. I tried baseball, but found it too boring. Lacrosse was great, but I got into it too late. Basketball was fun, but it was my best friend Mike Rosen's sport. Hockey was what I excelled at and by the time my family moved to Montreal for a year while my mother went back to university the sport dominated my existence.

Not only did I play the game, I was fixated on knowing everything about the sport. The only things I read were the sports pages and books about hockey. For a year or so collecting hockey cards and having them autographed by NHL players consumed my life. Once I snuck out of the house late at night to stand in front of the Bayshore Hotel in downtown Vancouver because I just had to have Joe Sakic's autograph. I waited in front of a Homer Street Italian restaurant for three hours to catch Wayne Gretzky.

In Montreal I had my first experience of "professional" hockey. Even though we were peewees (aged 12 and 13) we practised liked pros, we had our own fitness centre, equipment was provided free of charge and we traveled the province like conquering heroes, winning tournaments in front of adoring fans. At one tournament in Jonquière we even experienced "groupies" — two 12-year-old girls ran away from home to follow our team bus back to Montreal.

The glamour and the hard work were irresistible. We learned the importance of proper nutrition, fitness training and having a "winning" attitude. We wore ties and team jackets when we came to the rink for a game. We also learned the harsh reality that performance counts — the best players get more ice time and hence become even better.

At the end of the following season, back in Vancouver, I received my first invitation to a major junior evaluation camp and a year later, in second year bantam was scouted and then "listed" by a Western Hockey League team. In the end I only played a few major junior exhibition games and two seasons of junior A when I was seventeen, eighteen and nineteen. Given my abrasive style of play, I would probably have enjoyed significantly more success if I had been another few inches taller than my just-under six-foot frame.

Or maybe not. Because even though I loved hockey and occasionally even showed flashes of dominance, some things about the world of sport bothered me. And some things about me bothered the world of sport.

⊛ ⊛ ⊛ IN MY SECOND SEASON with the Chilliwack Chiefs of the B.C. Hockey League we were playing the Victoria Salsa, a young team that our coaching staff thought could be easily intimidated. A few minutes into the game, after a particularly energetic shift, the assistant coach came up behind me on the bench and said "Go at it in the first if you have to, but definitely in the second." I turned to look at him, but he was already looking away. I was surprised. It was the first time in my hockey career that I had been told directly to fight.

Not that I had anything against a little fisticuffs, or other forms of on-ice shit disturbing, but this just seemed too blatant, too constructed, not natural and it made me feel used, like a cog in a machine. Of course, I didn't fight at all that period or the next two. In fact, I didn't fight ever again for the Chiefs, because shortly thereafter, I told the coach I deserved some power play time and that my offensive skills were being underutilized. A few days later I was a member of the Castlegar Rebels.

● ● ● IN HINDSIGHT, the Rebels coach was right in his criticism: I was a dressing room lawyer. I did question his strategy, the way he conducted practices, his personnel choices, and I did stir up other team members against him. But I was right too: He was a poor coach. I had been around the game long enough, read enough books and experienced enough good coaches to recognize hockey smarts when I saw it. Not only did he not understand the capabilities of his players, but he was also an extremely poor technician. I loved a good, hard practice that made you feel a better player at the end of it — every coach I ever had agreed that was one of my strengths — but his were a waste of time. I was not invited back for the next season.

● ● ● SIGNED TO PLAY IN ROCHESTER, Minnesota, the following season I only lasted two weeks. Even though the coaching staff was more than capable, once again I was expected to provide muscle, once again I was not given an opportunity to show my offensive capabilities. Still, I was reasonably happy with the team until the day I was in the backyard with my billet. I couldn't believe my ears. "That nigger family moved in last month and this whole neighborhood is going downhill." It was only the second time in my life I had ever heard anyone talk like that — the first was when one of my peewee teammates had used the same word in a fight with a Seattle player and received a two-game suspension. I could have asked to change billets, but shortly after the incident, I was offered a spot in Nipawin, in the Saskatchewan Junior League, so I drove north, trying to recapture my focus and love for the game.

It was a good team, with a great coach, but I was feeling some severe culture shock. Half my new teammates chewed tobacco. Many made disparaging remarks about Native people, but for some reason what sticks out most in my memory is an incident at my billet's house where three of us were staying. It was game day, so we normally ate a meal of pasta about four hours before the puck was to drop. As I entered the kitchen to prepare my meal, I discovered one of the billet's teenage daughters already there, making the sauce for the three young men. "What's up?" I asked.

"My mother called me to come home and make pasta for you guys," she answered.

I could not believe it. Here I was, living in a world where young women were expected to drop whatever they were doing to cook for hockey players, who obviously were incapable of opening cans and cutting up a few vegetables. Sexism, racism and chewing tobacco — that's what I remember about my short stay in the Saskatchewan Junior Hockey League.

❂ ❂ ❂ I SPENT A FEW MORE WEEKS with the Powell River Paper Kings of the B.C. Hockey League, but my heart and brain were no longer in the game and in October of my nineteenth year I packed my hockey bag for the last time and headed off to confront the world outside of sport.

Don't get me wrong — I still loved the game. I just did not fit in. Or maybe it was simply that I wasn't good enough. Or that my mouth was too big. Or I'd been brought up the wrong way. Or a little of all of the above.

Whatever the reason, I faced a big change in my life. What to do? I still hadn't graduated from high school. My experience with the education system had, on balance, been unsatisfactory. The honest truth was I did not have a clue what to do with my life.

The only thing really going for me was a small pile of cash in the bank that I had saved up over the years from part-time jobs. So, I bought some travelers cheques and headed off to Europe.

The best things about travel are seeing the world and having the opportunity to think about where you have been. Over the next two years I visited a dozen or so countries, finished high school, did a couple of semesters of junior college, started reading for the first time in my life and thought a lot about just about everything.

● ● ● HOW DID I END UP at Concordia University? I certainly didn't choose it for its long tradition of student activism. In fact, the sole reason I applied for admission was that two of my best friends, Daniel and Michael Rosen were students at McGill University and I wanted to live with them in Montreal. I enjoyed my first semester, but didn't become involved in campus politics. It wasn't until I spent two weeks in Venezuela during spring break that my eyes were opened to the world of student activism.

The trip to Venezuela happened only because a very cheap last-minute ticket to Margarita Island was available on the day I looked for some place to go during my time off. I did not like the island — it's a tourist trap like many others — so I headed to the mainland where after a few days I ended up in the lovely colonial city of Merida.

Merida, about six hours from the Colombian border, is a town of just over 100,000, with almost 40,000 students. On my first day there I was out for a walk when I passed a large group of police congregating for no apparent reason. Naively I asked one cop what they were doing and he told me their presence was necessary because of a protest by university students a few blocks away. I decided to go over and ask the students what was going

Students were chucking large rocks at the police, which the police picked up and tossed right back

on. I quickly found them amidst raining rocks and burning tires blockading a road. I was told they were protesting plans to shut down the medical campus' cafeteria. Food for students at public university cafeterias in Venezuela costs only a nominal fee. The closing of the cafeteria would have forced medical students to travel to one of three other campuses around the city for their food. But the time it took to travel between campuses and eat was more than was available for their lunch break. So, in effect, medical students would have been forced to buy their own food. The system of (almost) free food for university students would be eliminated for them.

While the issues were interesting, the militancy of the protest was amazing and unlike anything I had ever seen before (or since, for that matter). A road was blocked with debris. Students were chucking large rocks at the police, which the police picked up and tossed right back. Some students were even throwing Molotov cocktails at the police, who responded with "la bomba" — teargas, my first experience with that noxious substance. Eventually, after a back and forth that went on for half an hour or so, the police pushed us (as I was now with the students) back onto the campus. Then everything just stopped. In Venezuela police need special authorization from the state governor to enter a university campus. This day's events were not considered of enough importance to warrant such special powers. Instead of entering the campus, the police simply launched canister after canister of teargas. Since the campus was quite small with a big cliff on the other side there was nowhere for us to go. To avoid suffocation from the gas we moved to the furthest edge of the campus and lay down on the ground where there was still a few feet of breathable air.

Given the scale of what I was experiencing, I naively assumed a revolution or something was just around the corner. But no. The clashes with the police simply ended at 5 p.m. when everyone packed up and left. Some of the more aggressive protesters told the police they would get them the following day and they did. The next day in the afternoon the whole thing started up again and was repeated every day until Carnival began.

My first experience with student activism was a strange combination of defending rights and good fun. When I got back to Montreal I decided to get involved at Concordia.

Why did I travel from hockey to political activism? My parents had always been involved in their unions, so I had some role models, but I think the most important reasons came from hockey. What I loved most about the sport was its passion. It feels good to devote yourself to a goal, whether that is to improve your skating, or read all there is to know about Noam Chomsky. It feels good to give yourself up to the game, whether that is scoring in overtime or chanting slogans at a demonstration. And then there's that other skill I learned in hockey: Being a dressing room lawyer. Or as I prefer to describe it: I honed my analytic skills and was willing to point out what I thought was right or wrong, for me, or my teammates. I just transferred what I learned from hockey to politics.

● ● ● PERHAPS ANOTHER REASON I went from playing hockey to student activism was because I never quite "fit in" or at least that was the feeling I had. Most of us probably feel that way at some time. Each of us has a different way of sticking out. Some of us are nerds, some of us are fat, some of us are gay, some of us are too tall, some of us are too short, some of us belong to minority religions, some of us are atheists, some of us of are too smart, some of us are not smart enough. One way I stuck out was because I was a

French Canadian in Vancouver and an "Anglo" in Montreal.

One of my earliest memories is of wishing my first name were different. Yves, which in English sounds like the "girl's name" Eve, was constantly mispronounced. Or adults would make a fuss about it. Other boys would tease me. I remember scoring goals and then having the rink public address announcer calling me "Ives" Engler. My name made me feel like an outsider. I think when you are made to feel like that you become more sensitive to injustice and unfair treatment whether aimed at you or others.

My first school, Ecole Anne Hebert, didn't help. It was a "programme cadre" school, to which French-speaking parents could send their children. The problem was that only my mother spoke French so my skill in that language was extremely limited. Since my older sister had successfully managed the transition into programme cadre, it was assumed I would as well. Unfortunately on my first day of school the kindergarten teacher spoke no English and was experiencing her first day of teaching. It was also her last day of teaching, at least in Vancouver. It seems that she had a nervous breakdown. In fact, to cope, she locked three of us boys in a closet. None of us were communicating well in French and we probably deserved some sort of punishment for being rowdy as five-year-olds can be. Still, it was not the best introduction to school and it did make me apprehensive about certain adults.

After a short time I was moved to a French immersion school for the rest of kindergarten and Grade 1. Then it was back to Ecole Anne Hebert for another try at more intensive French. This time I lasted a couple of grades.

While I eventually got comfortable being "French" at school it always seemed a bit weird in hockey, which was much more important to me than my academic career. Then, just to really confuse things, I moved to Montreal when I was ten because my mother had returned to university. All of a sudden I was an "Anglo" at a public school in Outremont (a wealthy French-Canadian inner suburb) where my mother sublet an apartment. My French was completely inadequate, which my teacher made clear in a way that demonstrated my stupidity to the entire class. Then, when I tried out for the top "Atom" level hockey team the coaches didn't even give me a good look; they shuffled me down to a second tier squad made up of players from Outremont and Town of Mount Royal. While I was a dominating player at this level, the background of most of my teammates was very upper class — their parents were mostly heads of corporations, business executives and lawyers. At both hockey and school I felt like an outsider. Things got so bad that after a few months I returned to Vancouver to live with my father.

So, when I returned to Montreal two years later with both my mother and father, I expected to hate the city once again. This time we lived on the Plateau, a mostly French working class part of the city. My mother switched me over to the Protestant school system so that I could attend a school in French, but with mostly recent immigrant classmates whose French was no better than my own. And the hockey was the best I ever experienced.

I tried out for and made the Double A team from Huron Hochelaga and it was hockey heaven! We practised or played almost every day. The coaching staff was fantastic. Everything was paid for because the association, whose enrollment area covered many of Montreal's poorest neighborhoods, owned a bingo parlor. But best of all, we were the best team in the city and one of the best in the province. (Of course it helped that Mike Ribeiro, future NHL star, was one of my teammates.) Because of our outstanding record we represented the Canadiens at the fabled Quebec Peewee Tournament, where we made the semi-finals, losing to the home

When you feel like an outsider in one way or another, you develop a critical outlook

team in double overtime in front of over 10,000 fans. Still, even though the coaches were great and I was playing on the top line by the end of the season, there was an undercurrent of resentment from some of the parents. I didn't quite belong. I was the "Vancouver Express" who took a coveted spot on the team from a local boy.

Then when I returned to Vancouver the following year and told stories of how great Montreal had been, my teammates treated me like I was the "Frenchy" from Quebec. It seemed like I was destined to be an outsider.

* * * PERHAPS EVERYBODY FEELS like an outsider at some time in her or his life. Among the many student activists I've met over the years, most have felt different, alienated in some way from the "normal" world. (Perhaps this is why so many of the activists at Concordia have been Muslims and Jews.) Being part of a minority religion or culture or viewpoint creates a sense of being on the outside looking in at the dominant culture or religion or point of view. When you feel like an outsider, in one way or another, you develop a critical outlook from that sense of "looking in." This can be a strength or a weakness. It can bring you closer to the truth, but it can also be a barrier between activists and "regular" people.

And strangely enough that has been the source of yet another feeling of being an outsider. Sometimes, as a former hockey playing jock who grew up in a neighborhood of longshoremen, electricians, secretaries, school teachers and the two elderly bookies who lived next door, I've felt like an outsider among the outsiders. Sometimes they seem too middle class, too artsy, too weird. Sometimes they seem disdainful of people like me. Sometimes I've felt too many activists look down on ordinary people, that they see themselves as superior to the crowd.

Then I think to myself, maybe all of us are outsiders in one sense or another. Maybe no one fits in completely, no matter where you are. And it sure is a lot more fun to be around people with a willingness to be different, to think critically, to strive for the truth, to challenge authority and try to make the world a better place. I'll choose that over boring old conformity any day.

I choose to conform with the non-conformists. I choose to be an insider with the outsiders. I choose to challenge authority, including the authority of those challenging authority.

CHAPTER THREE

THE IMPORTANCE OF SPEAKING TRUTH TO POWER

Once upon a time, during a great stock market boom, there lived a very powerful chief executive officer who thought so much of new clothes that he spent all his money in order to obtain them; his only ambition was to be always well dressed. He did not care much for his stockholders or his employees, and the latest video games did not amuse him; the only thing, in fact, he thought anything of was to go out and show a new suit of clothes. He had a coat for every hour of the day and as one would say of a billionaire "He is talking to his broker," so one could say of him, "The CEO is in his dressing-room."

The great city where he resided was very wealthy; every day many strangers from all parts of the globe arrived. One day, two swindlers came to this city; they made people believe that they were technological geniuses and declared they had invented the finest cloth to be imagined. Their colors and patterns, they said, were not only exceptionally beautiful, but the clothes made of their material possessed the wonderful quality of being invisible to any man who was unfit for his office or unpardonably stupid.

"That must be wonderful cloth," thought the CEO. "If I were to be dressed in a suit made of this cloth I should be able to find out which men in my company were unfit for their places and I could distinguish the clever from the stupid. I must have this cloth

The poor old CFO tried his very best, but he could see nothing at all, for there was nothing to be seen

woven for me without delay." He gave his blessing to an IPO that raised a large sum of money for the swindlers and his company purchased controlling interest in the start-up firm. The swindlers set up two research facilities and pretended to be hard at work, but they did nothing whatever in the lab. They asked for the most powerful computers, the finest silk, the most precious minerals and the latest in robotic technology; all they got they sold on the grey market and played video games on the fancy computers until late at night.

"I should very much like to know how they are getting on with the cloth," thought the CEO. But he felt rather uneasy when he remembered that he who was not fit for his office could not see it. Personally, he was of the opinion that he had nothing to fear yet he thought it advisable to send somebody else first to see how matters stood. Everybody in his company's management knew what a remarkable quality the cloth possessed and all were anxious to see how bad or stupid their fellow managers were.

"I shall send my honest old CFO to the weavers," thought the CEO. "He can judge best how the stuff looks, for he is intelligent and nobody understands his office better than he."

The good old chief financial officer went into the laboratory where the swindlers sat before the empty high tech weaving machines. "Heaven preserve us!" he thought, and opened his eyes wide, "I cannot see anything at all," but he did not say so. Both swindlers requested him to come near and asked him if he did not admire the exquisite pattern and the beautiful colors, pointing to the empty weaving machines. The poor old CFO tried his very best, but he could see nothing, for there was nothing to be seen. "Oh dear," he thought, "can I be so stupid? I should never have thought so and nobody must know it! Is it possible that I am not fit for my office? No, no, I cannot say that I was unable to see the cloth."

"Have you got nothing to say?" said one of the swindlers, while he pretended to be busy weaving.

"Oh, it is very pretty, exceedingly beautiful," replied the old CFO looking through his glasses. "What a beautiful pattern, what brilliant colors! I shall tell the CEO that I like the cloth very much."

"We are pleased to hear that," said the two weavers and described to him the colors and explained the curious pattern. The old CFO listened attentively, that he might relate to the CEO what they said and so he did.

Now the swindlers asked for more money, computers, silk and precious metals, which they required for weaving. They kept everything for themselves and not a thread came near the weaving machines, but they continued, as hitherto, to work at the empty looms.

Soon afterwards the CEO sent another honest board member to the weavers to see how they were getting on and if the cloth was nearly finished. Like the old CFO, he looked and looked but could see nothing, as there was nothing to be seen.

"Is it not a beautiful piece of cloth?" asked the two swindlers, showing and explaining the magnificent pattern, which, however, did not exist.

"I am not stupid," thought the member of the board "It is therefore my good appointment for which I am not fit. It is very strange, but I must not let any one know it." And he praised the cloth, which he did not see, and expressed his joy at the beautiful colors and the fine pattern. "It is very excellent," he said to the CEO.

Everybody in the multinational corporate headquarters talked about the precious cloth. At last the CEO wished to see it himself, while it was still on the loom. With a number of board members, including the two who had already been there, he went to the two clever swindlers, who now worked as hard as they could, but without using any thread.

"Is it not magnificent?" said the two old board members who had been there before. "Your eminence must admire the colors and the pattern." And then they pointed to the empty looms, for they imagined the others could see the cloth.

"What is this?" thought the CEO, "I do not see anything at all. This is terrible! Am I stupid? Am I unfit to be head of one of the world's largest corporations? That would indeed be the most dreadful thing that could happen to me."

"Really," he said, turning to the weavers, "your cloth has our most gracious approval," and nodding contentedly he looked at the empty loom, for he did not like to say that he saw nothing. All his fellow board members, who were with him, looked and looked, and although they could not see anything more than the others, they said, like the CEO, "It is very beautiful." And all advised him to wear the new magnificent clothes at the next corporate annual general meeting, which was soon to take place. "It is magnificent, beautiful, excellent," one heard them say; everybody seemed to be delighted and the CEO gave the two swindlers stock options worth at least $10 million.

The whole night previous to the day on which the annual general meeting was to take place, the swindlers pretended to work. People should see that they were busy finishing the CEO's new suit. They pretended to take the cloth from the loom and worked about in the air with big scissors and sewed with needles without thread and said at last: "The CEO's new suit is ready now."

The CEO and all his company's major shareholders then came to a hotel suite adjoining the ballroom where the annual general meeting was to take place; the swindlers held their arms up as if they held something in their hands and said: "These are the trousers!"

"This is the coat!" and "Here is the cloak!" and so on. "They are all as light as a cobweb and one must feel as if one had nothing at all upon the body; but that is just the beauty of them."

"Indeed!" said all the major shareholders; but they could not see anything, for there was nothing to be seen.

"Please undress," said the swindlers to the CEO, "that we may assist you in putting on the new suit before the large mirror."

The CEO undressed and the swindlers pretended to put the new suit upon him, one piece after another and the CEO looked at himself in the glass from every side.

"How well they look! How well they fit!" said all. "What a beautiful pattern! What fine colors! That is a magnificent suit of clothes!"

The organizers of the annual general meeting announced that it was time to begin.

"I am ready," said the CEO. "Does not my suit fit me marvelously?" Then he turned once more to the mirror, that people should think he admired his garments.

The corporate secretaries, who were to accompany the CEO, pretended to admire the suit; they did not like people to know that they could not see anything.

The CEO marched into the ballroom and all the managers and shareholders who saw him exclaimed: "Indeed, the CEO's new suit is incomparable! What a beautiful cloth! How well it fits him! We are going to make a fortune when this cloth goes to market." Nobody wished to let others know he saw nothing, for then he would have been unfit for his office or too stupid. Or even worse, all the company's money that had been invested in the new high-tech cloth would have been wasted and share prices would fall dramatically.

Just then, a group of chanting student activists, who had been demonstrating outside the hotel to protest the multinational firm's

"Hey dude, why are you standing up there naked?"

vast profits from making land mines and other military hardware, burst into the ballroom chanting "No War. No War. No War."

As surprised as the shareholders were by the intrusion, the protestors were even more startled by the sight of a naked CEO standing on the podium at the front of the ballroom pointing a finger at them.

"Hey dude, why are you standing up there naked? " one of the student activists finally blurted out.

"Cool," said another.

"Strip naked if you oppose war," shouted another, acting creatively to take advantage of the situation.

"That's it," said another. "Clothes off to protest militarism!"

Soon there were about twenty naked students. Company officials and security guards did not know what to do since, while the students were naked, so was their CEO.

Finally, everyone at the meeting also undressed and the student motion to end all military investment passed unanimously.

● ● ● OF COURSE, IN REAL LIFE, things often don't work out so well as in fables. For example, when that large crowd at Concordia University in Montreal confronted a former emperor from a far-away land about his naked use of power to destroy the lives of many poor people the former emperor's powerful supporters and a collection of professional flatterers, also known as the corporate media, were outraged. Friends and associates of the former emperor were so angry at the students that they:

• Demonized us as enemies of democracy and freedom in TV reports and newspaper columns (many of which were owned by the former emperor's friends) around the world. Slandered us with outrageous claims of anti-Semitism and violence.

• Banned discussion of the former emperor's part of the world.

Banned all demonstrations and political debates of any sort for months at the university, all in the name of defending the former emperor's right to free speech, which they claimed we violated.

• Called dozens of police to arrest one student (me) who challenged the ban. Threatened that student with arrest if he returned to campus the next day to take an exam.

• Banned members of Canada's Parliament from speaking on campus, to punish the students who so offended the former emperor's right to speak where and when he wanted.

• Organized a campaign of name-calling that flooded the student council offices with emails, letters and phone calls from around the world.

• Hired a film maker to make a "documentary" that was so one-sided in its condemnation of protesting students that media outlets not owned by the emperor's best pal laughed it off as blatant propaganda. The affront to basic journalism was shown repeatedly on the television network owned by the former emperor's best pal.

• Had flatterers who work for the former emperor's best pal write editorials in newspapers across the land demanding punishment and naming supposed "ringleaders" of the students.

• Laid criminal charges against a few students (most of whom beat the rap). Banned some prominent non-student activists from campus. Laid internal university discipline charges against a dozen students. Broke university and natural justice rules of fairness during the disciplinary process and coerced some members of the disciplinary committees to find certain students guilty.

• Suspended for one semester the elected media spokesperson of the student union. Banned that same student for another semester when he tried to attend student council to which he had been re-elected. Suspended that same student for five years when he insisted on his right to be on campus for board of governor and student council business — bodies to which he had been elected.

• Spent over a hundred thousand dollars from non-student sources to influence subsequent student union elections. This included full-page ads in national newspapers and extremely expensive telephone polling. Still some of the "bad" students were elected and re-elected.

● ● ● IN REAL LIFE there is usually a price to pay when someone speaks the truth to the rich and powerful. Still, I would argue, there is a much bigger price to pay if no one has the courage to do it: The world would never change for the better.

All of us are both individuals and members of society. Maybe I'm too young to understand this properly, but it seems to me that politics is ultimately about managing the relationships among our various roles. All of us are individuals, members of various groups, part of humanity and inextricably intertwined with nature. All sorts of formal and informal relationships have arisen throughout history to manage the conflicts that arise. Politics is all about building, testing, changing and destroying these relationships.

Challenging old ways is an essential element of politics. It is at the core of renewal. It is also the responsibility of youth. If we don't confront the established ways, who will? We have fresh eyes and energy. We have not yet learned to be stuck in the status quo. It is the job of every new generation to make authority justify its power and privilege. Blind acceptance of the way things are is the mortal enemy of progress.

Call me naïve, but I believe we can make a better world.

So, open your mind, take a look around and ask yourself: Why? Does this make sense? Is there some better way we could do that?

How do you get from a concern for the food you eat to developing an anti-capitalist perspective? It actually makes perfect sense when I look back on it.

Food was the first "issue" that got me thinking about how the world works. At a restaurant before a big peewee hockey game when I was 13 my coach Pierre told the team we could eat only spaghetti noodles and maybe a little tomato sauce (what he actually said was: "C'est seulement les nouilles de pates et peut'etre un peu de sauce aux tomates.") From that moment food became something I thought about. The idea that there was good food and bad food (my born-in-Montreal teammates were particularly fond of ordering "sauce" — brown gravy — over almost everything) captured my imagination. At hockey camps in subsequent years I attended workshops on the logic behind a good pre-game meal, the amount of water to drink on game days and how/why to replenish your energy right after the game. Paying attention to my hockey diet quickly morphed into general health awareness. I began reading about nutrition and exercise. As I started to lift weights and train in the summers my diet became a year-round obsession. I tried some supplements that were supposed to help build muscle mass, but didn't like them and the health risks worried me. Besides, they never seemed to work. I gravitated towards "natural" food and healthy eating. Things like sour cream, mayonnaise and red meat were more or less eliminated from my diet.

Soon I questioned everything I ate. This meant reading and talking about nutrition. As I came into contact with environmental food activism I realized that not only were animal products often unhealthy but also that industrial farming practices were cruel to animals and hard on the environment. I learned that meat, compared to soybeans and other plants, is an inefficient source of protein. It takes much more land to raise animals for food than it does to produce the equivalent nutritional value by raising edible plants. It's not ecologically sustainable for the entire world's population to consume the quantities of meat we eat in Canada. Eventually health awareness merged with a number of social/political concerns to shape my thinking on food.

By the time I traveled to Mexico I had decided to avoid meat. My friend Michael Rosen and I would say: "Sin carne, por favor." On the streets and in the wonderful little restaurants this simple request drew weird looks. For most Mexicans if you have money you eat meat, especially when eating out, because it's a status symbol. The idea that two young Canadian men only wanted beans and no meat (but lots of yummy guacamole and salsa) on their tacos or papa rellenos (baked potato) seemed strange.

As we traveled further south not eating meat became less of an issue, because meat, as common food, became less available. That's another reason I rarely eat meat to this day: Solidarity with poor people in the Third World where vast tracts of land that should grow food for local consumption are given over to ranching, producing cattle for the wealthy and well fed instead of the poor and hungry. Guilt and the knowledge that a meatless diet is better for me, lead me to the path of vegetarianism.

Traveling in Guatemala you get the distinct feeling something

Then reading about the history
of the country really made me ill

is not right. Sure there are many problems in Mexico. Some Mexico City suburbs are intense shantytowns while others look as wealthy as anything in the USA or Canada and have armed men guarding them. When soldiers stop and check everyone on the bus you are reminded of the insurrections in Chiapas, Guerrero and elsewhere. But the situation in Guatemala is so much starker. A lot of little things add up to the bigger picture of a country where much of the population is just not valued by the system. The fruits and vegetables available in markets where ordinary people shop often aren't very good, despite the fertile land. It's because the good ones are exported, according to ordinary Guatemalans I spoke with. It was fun to join in with the kids playing football, but I worried that they'd step on glass or that my shoes would hurt their bare feet. On hot days a glass of orange juice was an attractive thought, but you'd be taking a chance on getting sick because the unfiltered water used to clean the glasses could make you sick. For many Guatemalans this was the least of their concerns since they didn't even have access to running water at home. Then reading about the history of the country really made me ill: Centuries of oppression aimed at the majority Mayan population; Decades of U.S. interference, including a CIA-sponsored coup when ordinary people tried to make their country a better place.

The north east of Guatemala — home to the great Mayan city of Tikal — was the end of three months of Latin-American travel. Less than 48 hours after leaving Tikal I was in the posh Los Angeles suburb of Malibu. The culture shock was intense and one is slapped in the face by the gross inequities of our world. While Guatemalans often don't have running water, proper housing or even basic footwear many people in the City of Angels spend huge sums of money on goods or services that can be charitably described as conspicuous consumption. For example, at Malibu's

Pepperdine University where I stayed for a night, some wealthy donor gave millions of dollars to the university so that every table in the cafeteria could have fresh flowers each day for 10 years. While flowers are essential, at least in nature, I can think of a few more useful things to do with the money.

✦ ✦ ✦ IT WAS HARD TO ENJOY all that Los Angeles has to offer when you know a short plane trip away an entire nation lives in poverty. It gets you thinking about why a country like Guatemala — home to the great Mayan civilization — is now so underdeveloped. You read about Spanish exploitation and the extreme marginalization of the indigenous majority by the colonial system. You think about the 1954 (CIA-directed) overthrow of democratically elected reformist president Jacob Arbenz that led to a murderous 36-year long civil war. You wonder if the poverty you have seen is the result of the international capitalist system's drive for cheap labor and commodity dependent societies. Questions inevitably lead to answers and you feel more and more that there must be something you can do to right this wrong. You look around and you find international solidarity movements like Students Taking Action in Chiapas, School of the Americas Watch, International Solidarity Movement and you read what they have to say.

The more you learn, the more you begin to feel the weight of the world's injustice. You look around, aware of international and domestic poverty; you are struck by the emptiness and anti-human quality of consumerism. How much money is put into the advertisements on buses, billboards, washrooms, telemarketers, TV, movies, festivals, Internet and elsewhere? Because of all the advertising and the status associated with mostly useless goods, many of us feel compelled to play the game.

Yet, I'd bet that an observer from another planet who saw this consumerism would probably say: "Why do they bother — it doesn't even look like fun." This is especially true about automobiles and the monster vehicles that people apparently desire. Look around and wonder why people in southern California spend so much of their time commuting to work or working to pay for their ability to commute (insurance, gas, repairs and car payments). Los Angeles looks like a city designed to make cars essential. If you can afford one you buy one. When I rode the bus in L.A., people mostly looked like those on buses in Mexico or Guatemala, plus many African-Americans.

Los Angeles and its sprawling suburbs are a carmakers' dream, but when curiosity got me reading, I learned that rather than being a product of unregulated growth, the city really was planned to be the way it is. Not by the people who live there, but by corporations with motives other than sensible urban planning. L.A. is the most famous example of car companies buying up public transit and running it into the ground. According to Colleen Fuller in *Caring for Profit* "Beginning in the 1920s, General Motors president Alfred Sloan and top company executives masterminded a scheme to create a consumer market for automobiles in the United States. At the time, nine out of 10 people relied on the trolley networks that crisscrossed cities around the country. GM first purchased and then dismantled the nation's trolley companies, ripping up tracks and setting bonfires composed of railcars. In thirty short years GM succeeded in destroying a mass-transit infrastructure that would cost many billions of dollars to resurrect — more money than municipal governments could raise.

"The trolley cars were replaced with GM's diesel fuel buses, service was cut back, air pollution increased and people began buying cars. National Car Lines (NCL), a company controlled and funded by GM, soon operated public transit in 80 cities. A propaganda campaign — including the slogan "What's good for General Motors is good for America" — was mounted, depicting private automobiles as a modern, timesaving alternative to supposedly inefficient, slow, public transportation systems defended by behind-the-times municipal authorities and citizens."

After all was said and done, GM was found guilty of conspiracy for their actions in destroying public transportation. Nevertheless, GM continued to push the restructuring of the transportation landscape. According to Fuller, "In the 1950s the powerful American highway lobby launched an aggressive campaign for public funds to underwrite the construction of an Interstate road system. Charles Wilson, GM's president at that time, was appointed secretary of defence in 1953, and he argued that a national highway system was a national security issue. Federal highway administrator Francis DuPont, a member of GM's largest shareholder family, was given a green light and $50 billion to begin construction on the Interstate highway system. Across the United States, people fought plans to build freeways through their towns and cities, but Washington's ear was attuned only to the corporate sector." Similar forces have shaped the urban landscape across Canada.

● ● ● AND IT'S NOT JUST HISTORY. In 2003, three of the five biggest advertisers in the U.S. were car manufacturers. Perhaps that explains the curious fact that there are more cars than people of driving age in the USA. Surely it's more cost effective to call a cab when a breakdown occurs rather than having a backup vehicle? Or have the robots learned to drive? But, who cares? It's only important that the private automobile has been the single most important source of capitalist profit for nearly 100 years. What other explanation do we need? Please ignore the pedestrians and environment.

We continue to build more and more roads for more and more cars even though we know it's not ecologically sustainable. A decade after the first Earth Summit in Rio, another 2.4 percent of the world's forests were cut down while fossil-fuel consumption and carbon emissions rose sharply. Inhabitants of the U.S. and Canada are the largest and second-largest greenhouse gas emitters in the world (5.6 and 5 tons per person annually respectively) while the "Global South's" average is 0.7 tons. Because of this mostly northern abuse it is now estimated that worldwide temperatures will increase between 1.5 and 6 degrees Celsius this century. The Guardian weekly reports that "the earth is warmer now than it has been any time in the past 2,000 years, the most comprehensive study of climatic history has revealed."

So why do we continue down this path when it's clearly not sustainable? Do we enjoy the thought of a barren planet? Or is there something about our economic system that leads to ecological destruction? My reading and thinking about the subject convinces me that this is the correct answer.

● ● ● I BELIEVE THAT OUR SYSTEM of property rights, whereby a wealth-holding minority controls the means of production (factories, banks, etc.) leads to this callous disregard for the environment. Corporations and the wealth-holding minority benefit from externalizing costs. This means that they take the profit and society pays the ecological costs. For example, a logging company that clear-cuts all the logs around a community does not have to worry about the long-term ecological damages to the community; they can simply transfer their profits to another locale leaving the community with the ecological degradation. On the other hand, if the community controlled its own resources one would think it would take into account the long-term environmental costs of logging.

Our economy seems hooked on building more and more things that fewer and fewer people really need

The capitalist system also seems to thrive best with conspicuous consumption, at least in some parts of the world. Under capitalism, if consumers in the industrialized economies don't consume at an ever-increasing rate, the system falls into recession. Our economy seems hooked on building more and more things that fewer and fewer people truly need, while ignoring the real needs of billions of our fellow inhabitants of earth.

Capitalism's need for short-term profits is another factor that damages the environment. Corporations are legally required to maximize profits and that is calculated quarterly. Investors demand immediate results to drive up the price of the stock. But environmental sustainability is based upon long-term planning. Decades and centuries and even millennia are the measurements that matter for the planet's health.

Shouldn't our governments know this and act accordingly? But governments are beholden to the wealthiest and most organized in society and overwhelmingly these tend to be business interests. Take the Kyoto agreement, which is an extremely small step towards a reduction in green house gas emissions, as an example. The majority of Americans want their government to sign that agreement and design other environmentally friendly policies. The reason the U.S. administration has not signed Kyoto is simply because of the inequity of power within society. The business class, especially the auto and energy industries in this case, is sufficiently organized to block it. Yet, the working class, the "middle class" — or whatever you want to call the majority — is not sufficiently organized to force the government to sign on.

❀ ❀ ❀ BUT PRIVATE PROFIT isn't the only cause of ecological destruction. The biggest polluter in the U.S. is not a corporation but rather the U.S. military. "According to the Environmental

Protection Agency, unexploded ordnance waste can be found on 16,000 military ranges across the U.S. and more than half may contain biological or chemical weapons. In total, the Pentagon is responsible for more than 21,000 potentially contaminated sites and, according to the EPA, the military may have poisoned as much as 40 million acres, a little larger than Florida." The military can receive waivers from most U.S. environmental laws in the name of national security.

National security gives the military carte blanche to do all kinds of exciting things. Dolphins are trained as "frogmen" and used as bomb carriers against enemy submarines. Low frequency acoustic sonar for detecting submarines is used regardless of the harmful effect on sea creatures. (They've been known to cause the beaching of whales, resulting in their death.) Training in jungles with heavy machinery such as tanks and armored personnel carriers destroys sensitive eco-systems.

The military's foreign bases are also an ecological catastrophe. According to Foreign Policy in Focus, "[the U.S. military] violates international norms requiring governments to ensure that their actions do not harm other individuals or countries... Global peers (such as Japan and Germany) are able to force the U.S. to clean up its toxic messes, whereas little or no cleanup occurs in less developed countries, which have neither the resources and the technology to redeem the toxic bases nor the clout to force DOD [Department Of Defense] to do so.... The Army estimates that cleanup of all U.S.-caused soil and groundwater pollution overseas could cost more than $3 billion."

There's also a long history of the U.S. and other militaries using toxic substances that damage the environment and health of people in countries they attack long after they've left. The U.S. used chemical weapons such as napalm and Agent Orange during the Vietnam War and depleted uranium in the first Gulf War, all of which have had devastating human and ecological effects.

⬢ ⬢ ⬢ ANYONE WHO THINKS ABOUT IT knows that wars and militarism are horrible for the environment (including people). But are we doing anything about it? The recent trend seems to be expanding the scope of the problem. The U.S. military, with spending the size of the world's next 25 biggest armies, has a budget that is growing much faster than the rate of inflation. It's also expanding geographically. According to the Defense Department's 2003 "Base Structure Report" the Pentagon currently owns or rents 702 foreign bases in some 130 countries and has another 6,000 bases in the U.S. and its territories. However, Chalmers Johnson, author of *The Sorrows of Empire: Militarism, Secrecy, and the End of the Republic*, claims that "if there were an honest count, the actual size of our military empire would probably top 1,000 different bases in other people's countries." There are about 250,000 uniformed personnel on these bases with an equal number of dependents and other civilians. But for sections of the U.S. elite this is not enough. Their stated goal is to dominate the world by force and so we can expect the continued expansion of the U.S. Empire.

After invading Afghanistan the U.S. ended up with 13 more bases in that part of the world, which might have something to do with the Caspian Sea oil pipeline and getting a foothold in Russia's backdoor. Already there are new bases in Iraq, again not far from oil wells. Also it appears that West Africa — a region that is supposed to increase its oil exports as a share of U.S. imports from 15% to 25 percent by 2015 — will be home to some new bases. In 2003, the Bush administration gave the Colombian government $98 million to protect a portion of a "500-mile pipeline that last year was a frequent target of guerrilla attacks." (Washington Post)

Not coincidentally the pipeline transports 100,000 barrels of oil a day for Occidental Petroleum of Los Angeles.

None of this should be surprising since there is often a relationship between the location of foreign military bases and certain corporate interests, especially the energy sector. Capitalist interests and militarism are interconnected with both leading to a disregard for our environment. Militarism is not only hard on the environment but it is devastating to social systems. War is the ultimate failing of our ability to cooperate. Shouldn't there be a better way to deal with conflict?

Conflict seems most often driven by corporate interests, be it the military-industrial complex, energy companies or the broader corporate world. And wars are almost always fought by working people from one land against the working people of another. Those who have something to gain from conflict rarely fight. Invariably the death and destruction is in the interests of nations' ruling elite, not of ordinary people. Of course, usually there's some noble reason presented about the struggle for democracy or freedom. But just because politicians say it doesn't make it so.

Food, poverty, consumerism, ecology and war — things we confront every day but that I had never really thought about — got me reading and talking about the economic and social systems that dominate our lives. It seems clear to me now that we need some radical change.

CHAPTER FIVE

MORE GOOD REASONS TO BE AN ACTVIST:
INEQUALITY AND TRADE

As I traveled around Latin America, learned Spanish and studied the history of the USA's backyard I became troubled and then motivated to learn more. The more I read and thought about what I had seen, the more I felt like something needed to be done. The generations before us have done a really lousy job in so many ways in the lands of our southern neighbors. While I'd never claim to have all the answers, the problems are obvious, yet powerful interests, who prefer the status quo, block solutions.

● ● ● THE 50-YEAR-OLD MAN seated next to me on the plane from Mexico City to Tijuana seemed nervous. On the first leg of the trip to Monterrey he didn't say much, but then he began to tell me about himself. He was a farm worker from a small town near Cuernavaca and he was going to Tijuana to try his luck at crossing the border into the United States. He had a cousin in Los Angeles who would help him, but he had no plan (that he would tell me) to get there. Not only had he never been to the United States, he really didn't seem to have any understanding about the problems he was about to encounter. His family had remained at home and his goal was to get a job in the United States and send them money. The conversation was friendly and easy going until

Do trade agreements and economic liberalism spur growth and development?

he asked me how I was going to cross the border. When I told him that wasn't a problem for Canadians he seemed troubled and became distant. Or maybe I felt guilty. Maybe I felt that life is unfair to so many people.

● ● ● WE'RE TOLD THAT FREE TRADE is the solution to the problems of the underdeveloped world, including Latin America, but where is the evidence that open borders by themselves bring benefits to the world's poor? Do trade agreements and economic liberalism spur growth and development? Do the prescriptions of the International Monetary Fund, the World Trade Organization and other such organizations give countries the prosperity needed to sustain social programs and create jobs? Based on what I've read and seen the answer is no. Certainly the evidence suggests that the plight of the world's poor has never been the primary concern of the politicians, rich people and business councils who've backed economic liberalism, now usually called neo-liberalism. (Neo-liberalism can be defined as an opposition to social spending, idealization of a de-regulated capitalist marketplace and the claim that reducing barriers to trade and inflation are sure-fire cures to economic ailments.)

Consider the case of Mexico, which has been the "beneficiary" of neo-liberalism in general and the North American Free Trade Agreement (NAFTA) in particular. How do you determine whether a country is better off or not? One easy way to judge is by looking at immigration or emigration. A country that is doing well attracts immigrants and a country that is doing poorly loses population.

In the early 1990s, 10 years after Mexico's 1982 peso devaluation and the beginning of the country's neo-liberal economic restructuring, the flow of "illegal" migrants to the U.S. had become a political issue in the USA. Between 1980 and 1990 the number of Mexican-born people in the U.S. almost doubled from just over two million to more than four million (NY Times Dec.27, 2003). A large number of the Mexicans were un-documented and an easy target for xenophobic U.S. politicians. So, before Mexico entered NAFTA, proponents of the accord proclaimed that its growth-inducing properties would curb the flow of northbound migration. The argument put forth was that NAFTA would boost Mexican growth, which would create jobs and with more jobs Mexicans wouldn't need to seek work in the USA. So, what happened?

NAFTA did create hundreds of thousands of jobs in "free trade" zones (Maquiladoras), mostly assembly-type work in the electronic and consumer goods industries, generally in the north of the country, along the U.S. border. By 2000 some 700,000 Maquiladora jobs had been created. But, three years later, 300,000 of those jobs had disappeared due to the downturn in the U.S. economy and, more importantly, Chinese competition (NY Times, Dec. 27, 2003). With China's entry into the WTO in 2001, international capital, which underpins the Maquiladora sector, reckoned that Chinese workers could be paid a third the rate of a Mexican worker (50 cents U.S. per hour compared with a $1.47 hourly average [La Presse, January 12, 2003]). So the assembly lines were moved across the Pacific Ocean.

How has neo-liberalism affected migration patterns? When NAFTA was signed there were 2.4 million undocumented Mexicans in the USA, yet by 2003 that number had more than doubled to 4.81 million (NY Times, Dec. 27, 2003). The total number of Mexican-born people in the U.S. also doubled to about nine million from 1990 to 2000 (Globe and Mail, Jan. 3, 2004). Some might argue that this migration was due to the abundance of jobs created during the late 90s economic boom in the USA. But then how does one explain the continued, and even increased, migration as the U.S economy shed millions of jobs in 2001 and 2002? In fact, 2001 and 2002 were the two biggest years to date for "illegal" migration with more than 600,000 Mexicans going north in 2002 alone (Wall Street Journal, Oct 20, 2003). From 2000 to 2004 the number of undocumented workers in the USA increased from 8.4 million to 10.3 million, according to the Pew Hispanic Center.

This increased migration continues even as crossing the border has become more difficult, expensive and dangerous. Since the implementation of Operation Gatekeeper the number of U.S. border patrol agents has steadily increased from just over 3,000 in 1993 to some 9,000 in 2002 (WSJ, Oct 20, 2003). In addition, a huge fence was built in California, which forced migrants into the deadly Arizona desert. One result of the increased clampdown is more money going to the so-called "coyotes" who help migrants cross the border. The money available in the "coyote" trade has spurred an increasingly violent network of organized crime that has some comparing the border control situation to the futile war on drugs. Demand is so great that no matter how many "coyotes" are captured new ones appear.

The most important result of Operation Gatekeeper has been its effect on migrants. During the 2003 dying season, the hot summer months in the Arizona desert, some 200 people perished trying to cross the border. "The immigrants must walk at least three days through a death trap 450-kilometers long and 80 deep, ... it is the worst border in the western world and the deadliest across land anywhere." (Globe and Mail, Sept. 20, 2003)

Why do so many Mexicans risk it? Certainly not for the adventure. The man I sat next to on a flight from Mexico City to Tijuana wasn't looking forward to being away from his family; the very thought of sneaking across the border made him nervous. In

Montreal, Concordia's immigrant night-cleaners have told me they would prefer to be with their families. People leave their homes and families because they feel it is their best or only choice.

A flood of subsidized U.S. exports and reductions in subsidies have devastated the Mexican agricultural sector, especially small farmers. During NAFTA's first decade some 2.5 million Mexican farmers were driven from their land (Liberation, Jan 1, 2004). And for naïve city folk like myself who might see farm work as a chore it is not just a matter of Mexicans wanting to get off the farm. In the 10 years between 1989 and 1998 the percentage of U.S. farm workers, mostly Mexicans, without legal working documents increased from less than 10% of the farm worker population to over 50 percent (WSJ, October 10, 2003). This increase in un-documented farm workers has benefited U.S. agri-business, the source of the products undermining small farmers in Mexico. U.S. agricultural wages fell from $6.98 per hour in 1989 to $6.18 in 1998 in constant 1998 dollars (WSJ, October 10, 2003).

Outside of the agricultural sector, NAFTA has not been as bad, but certainly not great. Decent paying manufacturing jobs that support entire families are fewer now than when the NAFTA agreement was signed (Financial Times, July 1, 2003). Real wages for Mexican manufacturing workers have dropped significantly since NAFTA went into effect (USA Today, Dec. 31, 2003). And the situation is likely to get worse before it gets better as China's economy continues to expand.

● ● ● MEXICO'S ECONOMY isn't in a total free-fall though, which is testament to an ability to do what neo-liberalism seems to value above all else: export. The only problem is that in Mexico's case the exports are not products or materials, but people. Money sent home (remittances) from the U.S. has surpassed tourism and foreign direct investment as the second biggest source of foreign currency after oil. About $13.4 billion was remitted in 2003, 35% more than 2002. (www.dallasfed.org) The estimate for 2004 was over $16 billion.

To put this number into perspective lets add the likely combined wages of all 700,000 Maquiladora jobs created during the first seven years of NAFTA. Assuming 700,000 workers work 50 hours a week for 52 weeks a year at $1.47 per hour, the total amount brought into the Mexican economy is $2.68 billion. That's about the amount remittances increased between 2002 and 2003.

Victor Hanson, a professor at Cal State Fresno argues that "Mexico... stays afloat by exporting human capital [remittances]. If you shut that border down, in five years you'd have a revolution, because Mexico can't meet the aspirations of its own people." (L.A Times, July 20th, 2003) And you can bet Mexican politicians understand this fact. The same issue of the L.A Times reports that, "the migrants who come north used to be regarded as sellouts or deserters in Mexican society. Now, they are heroes praised by Mexican president Vicente Fox for the money they inject into that faltering economy."

So, NAFTA and its economic liberalization agenda has increased, rather than decreased, the flow of Mexican emigrants — convincing evidence neo-liberalism has not solved that country's economic woes. But, let's be clear. NAFTA has benefited some. Mexico has had a huge increase in billionaires. Some agri-business has done well. Large segments of the country's business elite and professional classes have grown wealthier. And certainly a few multi-nationals aren't complaining. Unfortunately, most Mexicans aren't members of these sectors of society.

● ● ● NOT ONLY DOES "GLOBALIZATION" not seem to work,

In other words, the favored part of the WTO is that which limits competition

it also doesn't really mean free trade. In fact, a central plank of free trade agreements is exactly the opposite of "free" trade. Rich countries are trying to impose trade rules that mean lesser-developed economies can no longer use a significant aspect of their competitive advantage when trading with richer countries. While advocates of the WTO and other corporate-sponsored global treaties claim economic advancement will result from increased international competition, in fact they are set on a course that would undermine free markets by increasing monopolies through strengthened patent protection.

What is a patent? Essentially it is a law that gives a monopoly for a set period of time to a corporation (or individual) with enough resources (sometimes creativity) to "invent" something. A patent becomes a legal piece of property that can be bought, sold or traded.

A central goal of the WTO, through the Trade-Related Aspects of Intellectual Property Rights TRIPs agreement, is to harmonize "upwards" the world's patent protection to those of the U.S. The reason G7 nations are proponents of the TRIPs agreement is because it will be benefit corporations based in the world's richest countries. The World Bank estimates that if a global agreement on intellectual property rights goes fully into effect the developed nations would gain the most with the U.S., Germany, Japan and France combined standing to gain $34.9 billion US annually — mostly at the expense of China, Mexico, Brazil and others. Some claim that the U.S. would abandon the WTO if it weren't for the TRIPs agreement. In other words the favored part of the WTO is that which limits competition.

It's not only at the WTO where anti-competitive monopolies reign. The Central American Free Trade Agreement between the U.S. and Central American countries also has a focus on increased patent protection. The Bush administration is demanding these countries increase their patent protection beyond even the 20 years mandated under U.S. law. Increased patent protection is also at the forefront of Free Trade Area of the Americas negotiations, as it was when Mexico signed the NAFTA. These agreements, as well as other bi-lateral agreements the U.S. may sign, will supersede the recent WTO agreement on drug patent relaxations, making the WTO agreement on AIDS and other epidemic diseases meaningless for many poor countries.

Canadians have also been caught in globalization's patent net. As a secret document released in 2003 reveals, the Mulroney Conservative government, with a nudge from the Reagan U.S. administration, increased patent protection from 17 to 20 years prior to signing the first free trade agreement. Similarly, the Canadian government succumbed to a WTO decision and banned the stockpiling of generic drugs in anticipation of the end of a patent. Skyrocketing drug costs that harm Canadian healthcare are the result.

But surely patents just make sense? Perhaps, but Europe and North America were "free" from this kind of limit on trade when they industrialized. During the 19th century, when western European nations were competing to develop their economies, innovation often meant "stealing" the best ideas from neighbors. This facilitated competition and innovation. Backward economies could leap ahead by the creative use of the latest technology. But, as rich countries outsource manufacturing, patents are becoming ever more important to G7-based corporations. U.S. patents issued per year have nearly tripled over the past two decades. Rather than building a system that will encourage growth and innovation, we are writing rules to ensure the dominance of a few large corporations based in the world's richest countries.

Even worse, as part of the patent expansion process multinational corporations are increasingly devising mechanisms to steal poorer countries' indigenous and cultivated intellectual property. One of the leading authors on the subject, Indian activist Vandava Shiva writes: "Biopiracy is the theft of biodiversity and indigenous knowledge through patents. It creates a false claim to novelty and invention, even though the knowledge has evolved since ancient times. Diverting scarce biological resources to monopoly control by corporations is resource theft from the poorest two-thirds of humanity who depend on biodiversity for their livelihoods and basic needs — it creates market monopolies and excludes the original innovators from their rightful share of local, national, and international markets.

"Instead of preventing this organized economic theft, WTO rules (and other trade agreements) protect the powerful and punish the weak. In a dispute initiated by the United States, the WTO forced India to change its patent laws and grant exclusive marketing rights to foreign corporations on the basis of foreign patents. Because many of these patents are based on biopiracy, the WTO is in fact promoting piracy. Over time, the consequences of TRIPs for the South's biodiversity and southern people's rights to their diversity will be severe. No one will be able to produce or reproduce patented agricultural, medicinal, or animal products freely, thus eroding livelihoods of small producers and preventing the poor from using their own resources and knowledge to meet their basic needs of health and nutrition."

In fact, corporations don't lobby for "free" markets; instead they lobby for patent controls to drive up their profits. For instance, between 1975 and 1994 Microsoft averaged four patents a year while between 1995 and 2000 the annual average increased to 240 (Canadian Business, Sept. 2, 2003). IBM in 2001 was awarded a record 3,411 U.S. patents, the most awarded to any patent holder and nearly 20% more than in 2000. The company now holds over

37,000 patents worldwide (www.pc.ibm.com/us/why). The pattern is clear; over the past 20 years the number of patents issued annually in the U.S. has nearly tripled (www.patentmatics.com/pub72.htm). By 1902 the U.S. patent bureau had given out one million patents; by 2002 five million and this was expected to increase to seven million by the end of 2004! (Canadian Business, Sept. 2, 2003)

Corporations that clamor for the "free market" when it comes to regulating their activities and when they want to ship their goods across borders are often claiming seemingly unnecessary patents in case they are useful (profitable) later on. This is one way corporations maintain control over "their" industry. Patents that are not profitable for one company will frequently be licensed to another. Canadian Business reports that, "revenues from (patent) licensing soared in the U.S. from $15 billion US in 1990 to more than $110 billion in 1999." (Sept. 2, 2003)

The creation in 1982 of the U.S. Court of Appeals for the Federal Circuit has been much more favorable to patentees (as its advocates had foreseen). According to patent critic William W. Fisher III: "Until the 1980s, both the Patent Office and the courts resisted the patenting of software programs, primarily on the ground that they constituted 'mathematical algorithms' and thus were unpatentable 'phenomena of nature.'

"In 1981, the United States Supreme Court signaled a slight weakening in this resolve, upholding the patent on a software program (embedded in a computer) that served to monitor continuously the temperature inside a synthetic rubber mold. Since that time, the Federal Circuit has adopted an increasingly receptive posture; today, virtually any software program (if novel, nonobvious, etc.) is patentable, so long as the applicant describes it as being programmed into a general-purpose computer. The predict-

Today, most creation is collaborative and controlled by large corporations

able result has been an enormous surge in software patent applications." (http://eon.law.harvard.edu/property99/history.html)

Just like the notion that capitalist globalization is about free markets the image of the lone scientific inventor in her garret is almost wholly obsolete. Today, most creation is collaborative and controlled by large corporations. Corporations have a "monopoly of monopolies" (as an aside, patents were originally meant as a mechanism to protect the lone creator from overpowering corporations). Equally important, the extent to which every creator depends upon and incorporates into her work the creations of her predecessors is becoming ever more obvious. According to Fisher, "like other 'monopolies' patents and copyrights were [are] dangerous devices that should be deployed only when absolutely necessary to advance some clear public interest." (http://eon.law. harvard.edu/property99/history.html)

One reason for the rise in drug costs and the resulting immense profitability of pharmaceutical companies is the strengthening of patent protections by the U.S. government in 1984. Similarly, thousands if not millions go without life-saving generic drugs to protect the drug industry's sacred patents.

The U.S. Supreme Court's decision in 2003 to uphold copyright extension is yet another reminder of how corporate monopolies are increasing. In 1998 major players in the entertainment industry such as Disney, which was about to lose its Mickey Mouse stranglehold, lobbied Congress to increase copyright. It was extended by two decades to 95 years for corporate copyright and individual copyright was increased to 70 years after the creator's death. This decision was only one of many in the trend towards strengthening copyright. Over the past 40 years Congress has increased copyright 11 times. (NY Times, October 14, 2002)

In effect, what we are seeing with increased patent protection and other aspects of so-called free trade is an attempt to bolster the system where poor people in most of the world can be super-exploited for the benefit of a tiny minority of rich and powerful people who own or control most major corporations. Anyone who believes, like I do, that all people are members of the same human family, must work to create a fairer world. That is why Concordia students played a small part in organizing the anti-FTAA (Free Trade Agreement of the Americas) demonstrations in Quebec City. That is why we march when trade ministers and heads of state meet, wherever they meet. For people who care, it's the least we can do.

CHAPTER SIX

ANOTHER GOOD REASON TO BE AN ACTVIST:
HEALTH

Playing hockey and health go together like playing the stock market and money: you can't have one without the other and being interested in the latter is a necessity for the former. To be successful in competitive sports you need to learn about many aspects of health such as nutrition, physiology, exercise science, psychology, rehabilitation and how to deal with physicians, surgeons, chiropractors, physiotherapists, psychologists and other practitioners. Of course, living with a mother who was nurse and then went on to become a professor of epidemiology likely also affected my interest in the subject. Whatever the reason, a concern about health was also a part of what turned me towards activism.

The dominant attitude inside the health "system" seems to be: Got an illness? Medicine can cure it. The list of "cures" is almost endless. Drugs, heart pumps, MRIs, CAT scans, a thousand different surgical procedures, an endless variety of specialists, etc. — the modern medical system has got it all. If medicine can't cure it today, it's only a matter of time, or money, for research to solve the problem. Soon human genomics will allow us to isolate all disease-causing genes. In some not-too-distant future medicine will be able to cure all our ailments.

Yet there is little evidence to suggest that curative medicine has greatly improved people's health

Should we believe these proclamations? What does history have to say? Do medical technologies have any downside? And what interests profit from these claims?

● ● ● HEALTH CARE ECONOMICS AND POLICY are complicated, especially in rich countries. Healthcare expenditures comprise about 15% of the U.S. economy, 10% of the Canadian and 8% of the British. In the political realm healthcare policy is consistently atop the agenda.

But what impacts human health — for good or bad — is not simply the narrowly defined health sector. In fact, almost certainly our health is determined less by healthcare expenditures than it is by the rest of the economy and other social/political determinants. Still, most health news focuses on curative medicine, which happens to dominate modern medicine to a greater or lesser degree in every industrialized nation.

Yet there is little evidence to suggest that curative medicine has greatly improved people's health. Conversely, human wellbeing has been positively impacted by public health promotion. While estimates on the issue vary, health experts agree that the majority of life expectancy improvements over the past century are the result of public health promotion not curative medicine. At one end of the spectrum, Laurie Garrett in *Betrayal of Trust* estimates that "86 percent of increased life expectancy was due to decreases in infectious diseases. The same can be said for the United States, where less than 4 percent of the total improvement in life expectancy since the 1700s can be credited to twentieth century advances in medical care." Others disagree with her enthusiasm for public health promotion, but there is a general agreement that prevention is what works.

But what the heck is "prevention" and what is "cure"?

We sometimes hear that "an ounce of prevention is worth

a pound of cure", which is confusing since "prevention" has increasingly become synonymous with check ups — full body CT scans, cancer tests, etc. These technologies are meant to diagnosis a disease early so medicine can then cure it. But the essence of prevention is avoiding disease all together. The problem is, from a profit-oriented economic system's point of view, there's big money to be made selling and administering "preventive" medical technologies and little in public health promotion. Major companies such as General Electric and Johnson & Johnson sell billions of dollars worth of "preventive" technologies that are really nothing more than entry points into the curative medicine establishment.

Not surprisingly, these companies do whatever they can to expand their markets. At the end of January 2004 England's Observer newspaper reported that "a clutch of famous women, including Liz Hurley, Caprice and Carol Vorderman ... [were] duped into supporting a sophisticated lobbying campaign secretly orchestrated from Brussels by one of the world's largest public relations firms" on behalf of U.S. biotech firm Digene. The actresses signed up to help in the fight against cervical cancer after "a group calling itself the European Women for HPV [human papilloma virus is linked to cervical cancer] Testing sent letters to influential women asking for support." Never was it mentioned that the group was a front for a company that "would make hundreds of millions of pounds if the [cervical cancer] tests were introduced in the UK." Similar, if less reported, practices are common within the medical "prevention" industry throughout the world.

In addition, doctors who are paid on a fee-for-service (in other jobs this is called piecework) basis make a profit from check ups. So they have a financial self-interest in defining "prevention" as a checkup or test. That's not all. Lesley Doyle in *The Political Economy of Health* explains that "power and prestige in medicine are allocated to a very considerable extent on the basis of scientific and technological innovation and on the extent to which particular specialists [doctors] are able to exercise their instrumental skills. ... Doctors are trained to see themselves as scientists, and, for the majority, job satisfaction is largely derived from the scientific and technological aspects of their work."

If it were only a matter of the difference in profit possibilities between public health promotion and medical devices or doctor's relationship to technology the word "prevention" wouldn't be so confusing, but there's more.

● ● ● PUBLIC HEALTH PROMOTION, to properly combat ill health, has to confront various entrenched corporate interests. Anti-smoking campaigns, for instance, run afoul of big tobacco companies. Serious anti-obesity activists challenge food companies' incessant advertising of larger portions of unhealthy foods and domination of the food market, not to mention the auto industry's (car, tire, steel, truck insurance, rubber, oil companies) 75-year-old push to expand auto sales through highway expansion and an ever-growing suburbia. You're not supposed to talk about the link between a lack of public transit, sensible (walk-able) urban planning and obesity. Anti-cancer activists are told "there's no problem" with the fact that companies release an average of two to five new chemicals into our environment each day, with little testing for safety or that worldwide production of chemical substances has increased from one million tonnes in 1930 to 400 million tonnes today. (Cambridge Quarterly of Health Care Ethics and Le Monde, Feb. 14, 2004) Even those who would promote public health through improved sewage, water systems, vaccine systems, education, health inspections and infection control — all of which require increased social spending (taxes) and so can be unpopular with wealth-owning classes — are forced to become political activists who challenge neo-liberal capitalism.

So who is going to promote public health? Certainly not the drug or medical device companies that profit from curing illness. Doctors whose wealth, knowledge and prestige are connected to curing as opposed to preventing ill health? The corporate community, a traditional supporter of curative medicine because it reduces the focus on preventive measures that challenge their narrow economic interests?

Throughout history governments, acting upon pressure from citizens, have done the most to advance public health. (Ironically it was, in large part, the success of public health promotion — improved sewage, food programs for the poor, etc. in the late 1800s and early 1900s — that allowed mainstream medicine to consolidate its emphasis on cure.) But governments are, for the most part, a reflection of the power dynamics within society so they will only take on the powerful drug companies, doctors and broader corporate world when under intense popular pressure to do so. On occasion they have. Unions have won some occupational health and safety laws, much to the dismay of many companies. Anti-smoking activists have won restrictions on smoking advertising, which Big Tobacco tries to subvert. To implement universal medicare Canadian governments not only challenged insurance companies but also doctors' associations. In 1962, doctors in the province of Saskatchewan, the birthplace of Canada's universal healthcare system, went on strike for 23 days to block medicare and other changes to their control over medicine. The doctors lost the battle against medicare but nonetheless maintained their fee-for-service payment system and much of their power within medicine. The American Medical Association has also for the last

U.S. life expectancy is lower than every other rich nation and some poor ones

75 years actively opposed government health insurance and only relented on seniors Medicare after a long battle. In other words activism has been the key ingredient in improving the system.

These victories have positively affected people's lives. Better workplace rules prevent injury death and disease, anti-smoking legislation reduces the number of new smokers and universal health insurance guarantees access to some level of healthcare. Victories, such as government health insurance, that wrestle some control over medicine away from the medical industry — doctors, private hospitals, pharmaceutical, biotech and apparatus companies —also lay the ground for further improvements in health policy.

The public health care system in Canada compared to the U.S., for instance, acts as a counterweight to the entrepreneurial focus on cures over prevention. Canada's "socialized" medicine, through more centralization and rational planning, does put an increased emphasis on public health. In most provinces vaccinations are provided in a more accessible and rational manner. Public health units are better equipped and quality public education is more widely available than in the U.S. because a publicly funded system does have a financial incentive to do what really works.

● ● ● AN IRONY THAT SEEMS TO HAVE ESCAPED the notice of the corporate health industry is that public health insurance actually makes the curative health system more efficient. The U.S. health system provides the clearest example of the exceedingly inefficient nature of a for-profit health industry — not to mention how ineffective it is at keeping people alive. U.S. life expectancy is lower than every other rich nation and some poor ones. U.S. health expenditures are by far the highest of any country in the world at 15% of GDP. No other country spends even 11 percent of GDP. The

U.S. also spends much more in absolute dollars. Americans pay about $5,000 on average for health coverage while Canadians, the fourth biggest spenders, shell out $3,000.

One commonly cited reason for the larger U.S. health bill is the lack of price controls on drugs. Price controls, however, are not the only reason U.S. drug prices are higher than the rest of the industrialized world. Another important reason is that U.S. governments have little control over the purchase of drugs, unlike in countries with universal healthcare. Government drug purchasing can drive down prices through bulk discounts. Not only are drugs more expensive in the USA, but residents of that country are the biggest pill poppers in the world, at least partly because of deregulated pharmaceutical industry advertising. In the USA pharmaceutical companies are free to charge whatever they can to recoup their highest-in-the-world advertising costs. The sheer lunacy of the "system" boggles the mind.

Another contributor to higher costs in the U.S. health system is the focus on expensive technologies that are not really of much use. Then there is the higher rate of unnecessary procedures. For-profit hospitals have a financial self-interest to perform medical procedures. So do fee-for-service doctors and specialists who completely dominate U.S. health care. Even in Canada some 90% of doctors are paid this way while in Britain the National Health Service pays most doctors a salary. Careful consideration of the efficacy of every test or treatment, which should underpin all medical evaluations, is too often overlooked when profits are to be had. And contrary to popular wisdom, curative medicine is not simply a good. Though often beneficial in the short term, curative medicine can also be detrimental to health. For instance, the Chicago Tribune calculated that in 2000 there were 103,000 deaths from hospital-grown infections. About 75% were preventable, mostly from better cleaning techniques by doctors and nurses. (www.researchprotection.org) According to a Canadian study, after discharge, 76 of 328 patients followed experienced at least one adverse event including two people who died. (CMAJ) The biggest barrier to hospital safety improvement? Our economic system, which focuses almost exclusively on cures and technology where the biggest profits are to be found. While billions of dollars are spent annually on the development of new drugs and medical technologies, little is spent on basic hospital infection control.

In addition, capitalist-driven curative medicine overlooks the importance of other social determinants in ill health. Lesley Doyle writes, "under capitalism… It is always individuals who become sick, rather than social, economic or environmental factors which cause them to be so."

Another significant contributor to U.S. health costs is the higher administrative cost associated with multiple insurers, each of which have their own bureaucracy and advertising expenses. Data reported in the New England Journal of Medicine shows that, adjusting for population, the U.S. spends $209 billion more every year on extra administrative costs than the Canadian single-payer (government) insurance system. The study didn't even take into account the additional 10 to 15 percent of revenue that is siphoned off as profit by insurance companies and profit-oriented hospitals.

Both U.S. and Canadian governments spend approximately the same on healthcare — in 2001, north-of-the-border governments spent 7 percent of GDP while American governments spent 6.7 percent. But, in the USA 80 million are without insurance at some point every year and in Canada that government spending provides health coverage for everyone. In the U.S. individual spending adds up to another 8.3 percent of GDP while in Canada it is 3 percent.

⊛ ⊛ ⊛ ACCORDING TO SOME ESTIMATES about 18,000 U.S. residents die each year as a direct result of being uninsured. Those who die are almost entirely the working poor. In addition, I would venture to guess that the stress that results from lacking health insurance causes thousands more to die prematurely.

Poverty and socio-economic status more generally are significant determinants of illness and life expectancy in every nation. There is good evidence to suggest economic inequality, which the lack of universal health coverage in the U.S. both re-enforces and is a manifestation of, contributes more to lowering life expectancy than the lack of health coverage. A growing body of evidence suggests that countries with lower levels of economic inequality have higher life expectancies. According to the Financial Times, "if you look for differences between countries, the relationship between income and health largely disintegrates. Rich Americans, for instance, are healthier on average than poor Americans, as measured by life expectancy. But, although the U.S. is a much richer country than, say, Greece, Americans on average have a lower life expectation than Greeks. More income, it seems, gives you a health advantage with respect to your fellow citizens, but not with respect to people living in other countries. We lack the data on the relative health of the richest tiers in different countries, but it would not be surprising if even the wealthiest Americans paid a personal price for their nation's inequality.

"The reasons are that once a floor standard of living is attained, people tend to be healthier when three conditions hold: they are valued and respected by others; they feel 'in control' in their work and home lives; and they enjoy a dense network of social contacts. Economically unequal societies tend to do poorly in all three respects; they tend to be characterized by big status differences, by big differences in people's sense of control and by low levels of civic participation."

Taking a look at Japan Dr. Stephen Bezruchka from the University of Washington explains: "Japanese men smoke the most of all rich countries. Yet they are the healthiest population on the planet. It seems you can smoke in Japan and get away with it. It's not that smoking is good for you, but that compared to other things, it isn't that bad. Smoking is much worse for you in the U.S. than it is for the Japanese in Japan, where the gap between the rich and poor is much less... Similarly, it isn't Japan's health care system that is responsible for its remarkable health. Anyone who has looked at their system will tell you it isn't much to write home about...Japan is a caring and sharing society that looks after everyone and that matters most for your health."

Health is intimately connected to people's psychological state. And inequality appears to harm people's psychological state.

● ● ● BUT IT'S NOT ONLY POVERTY and inequality within wealthy nations that leads to ill health. In Africa, Latin America and Asia, the lack of proper drinking water or sewage leads to the premature death of many millions every year. Every year 14 million people die from diseases for which medicines exist but are inaccessible (National Post, June 2, 2003).

The pharmaceutical industry only cares about those who've got cash, as the actions of a French company Aventis highlight. In 1995 Aventis suspended production of a substance that was effective against sleeping sickness, which kills hundreds of thousands every year, on the grounds that it was not profitable, but relaunched it after discovering that it was also effective in removing women's facial hair. More generally, medical research focuses on what is profitable. There is a serious global inequality of health resources. Public health officials use the term the "10/90 gap." In effect, the wealthiest 10 percent of the world receives 90 percent

According to the profit motive
90 percent of humanity is of little value

of all health research spending, while the poorest 90 percent only receives 10 percent. According to "MSF [Medecin Sans Frontieres], neglected diseases, which threaten the lives of tens of millions of people, mainly in Africa, accounted in 2002 for less than 0.001% of the $60-70bn spent a year on medical research throughout the world." (Guardian Weekly, June 5, 2003) According to the profit motive 90 percent of humanity is of little value. The roots of poor health within the very system of society, which are most obvious in non-industrialized nations, has led many doctors to put down their white coats and stethoscopes and join the struggle against capitalism and imperialism. Che Guevara and Salvador Allende are two of the best known.

⚬ ⚬ ⚬ SHOULD WE BE SURPRISED that so much of medicine is driven by the same interest as the rest of our profit-driven economy? If we are, it is only because we project our values, that medicine is about healing and nurturing, onto the medical industry. We forget that the only reason today's medical establishment appears even slightly humane is as a result of struggles by activists for regulation of medical practices. We overlook the fact that much of the medical industry, like capitalist enterprise in general, is structured to make a buck no matter the human, social or ecological costs.

But we can do better if we can just get more people active. The struggle to improve public health has an additional very important side effect. It can empower us to take more control over our own health. Lesley Doyle explains, "a just health service would not only have to provide equal access to medical care, but would also have to address itself seriously to such problems as how to demystify medical knowledge and how to break down barriers of authority and status both among health workers themselves and also between workers and consumers." (PEH) In other words, in the case of healthcare, activism is really an end as well as a means. One more reason to get involved.

CHAPTER SEVEN

UNDERSTANDING THE GAME YOU'RE PLAYING

It's all very well to look at the world around you, see the contradictions and get angry. But, in order to do something about it, to effect change, you must learn how the world works and why. The best place to start is where you are — in my case that was at university. So I spent some time trying to figure out the relations of power and the underlying causes for some of the apparently irrational behavior of the Concordia administration.

The experience of getting arrested was not a whole lot different than getting a penalty after a hockey fight. In both cases you get led away by an authority figure. In both cases the "event" is designed to motivate your team. In both cases you're most effective if you have a good understanding of the game. In hockey that means feeling the ebb and flow of the play, knowing your teammates, getting under the skin of the opposing players and attacking when the time is right. In student activism (maybe all politics) it means first of all understanding the big picture.

● ● ● I WAS ARRESTED FOR SETTING UP an information table, but underlying all that happened was the uncomfortable fact that student activism is not popular with many wealthy donors to Concordia. Often this activism threatens their interests directly. Or

In the wake of the Netanyahu affair,
at least one major Concordia donor backed out

sometimes corporations and wealthy donors simply don't like the volatile climate that student activism supposedly creates. Some important people just don't like the idea of students pointing out that "the emperor has no clothes."

In the wake of the Netanyahu affair, at least one major Concordia donor backed out. Some BoG members cited this as rationale for the clampdown on student rights. Marcel Dupuis, the university's director of corporate and foundation giving, conceded to the Montreal Gazette that "donors and alumni are saying, 'If you don't get things in order, we're pulling the funding.'" Later in the year, Rector Lowy further elaborated that there "have been repercussions already on fundraising."

That is why in the aftermath of the Netanyahu affair, BoG people decided that not only should students be blocked from all Middle East political discussion, but that the Rector be given the authority to expel students without due process. Also curious was the decision that all student information tables in the busiest corridors of the university were now a "fire hazard."

● ● ● OF COURSE, ADMINISTRATIVE CLAMPDOWNS on student protest are not solely a Concordia phenomenon nor are they new. However, they do seem to be increasing at campuses across North America. During the winter semester of 2003 the administration at Toronto's York University repeatedly displayed a disdain for student protest. President Lorna Marsden decided the best method to deal with anti-war protests was to call the police to break them up. In the summer of 2004 she simply banned a prominent activist (the courts later overturned the expulsion). In early 2005 police were called to break up an indoor protest, assaulting some students in the process. A few months after leaving office in 2003 former McGill (Montreal's other English-language university) principal

Bernard Shapiro explained how he treated political protest there during his 7-year tenure. "I decided that there would be no political demonstrations of any kind for anybody — if you want to demonstrate, that's fine, there's the public streets, but nothing on campus." McGill's new principal Heather Munroe-Blum later formalized the protest ban policy.

There have also been numerous reports about an increase of 'free speech zones' on American campuses. These Orwellian named zones effectively restrict protest to either small areas or parts of the campus far from student activity. The University of Central Florida's student newspaper explains: "UCF's policy keeps law-abiding protesters and activists from reaching the majority of the campus."

● ● ● ONE REASON FOR THE INTENSITY of the crackdown on student activism is the all-mighty dollar. Universities don't have enough of them and thus feel they must please those people with lots. In Canada, government spending on education dropped precipitously during the 1990s. It fell almost 25% from 7.7% of Canadian GDP in 1992 to 5.9% in 2001. According to Statistics Canada, between 1990 and 2000, government money as a percentage of the post-secondary education budget dropped from 69 percent to 55 percent. In the U.S., "state aid to public universities has been falling, now accounting for just 25% of the budget at the University of Wisconsin, 13% at the University of Virginia and a bare 10% at the University of Michigan." Overall, "state aid accounted for 36% of university budgets nationwide in 2000, down from 46% in 1980." (WSJ, April 18, 2003)

In large part, the drop in public funding and its negative effects on universities are a result of the process of corporate or neo-liberal globalization discussed previously. Central to the process of corporate globalization are "free" trade agreements, which in a more honest world would be known as free investment agreements.

Agreements such as NAFTA, World Trade Organization (WTO) and the proposed FTAA, which we were organizing against with that table I was arrested at in the ConU mezzanine, reduce governments' ability to fund social programs. These agreements give corporations and their wealthy shareholders increased power to demand lower taxes to "compete" with lower-taxed regions. This reduces governments' ability to tax corporations and their wealthy shareholders, thwarting the necessary redirection of this money toward social spending.

According to a Financial Times editorial, "since 1996 the average corporate tax rate across the 15 nations of the European Union has declined from 39 percent to just under 31.7 percent. [In 2005 further cuts in corporate taxes were announced in major European countries.] The story is similar among the 30 industrialized countries of the Organization for Economic Co-operation and Development, where the average tax rate has fallen from 37.5 to 30.8 percent. The reason: Competition." (May 2, 2003)

Governments have entered a race to attract businesses by driving down the rates at which they levy tax on companies. Similarly, there has been a reduction in personal income taxes, disproportionately to the benefit of the wealthy. These reductions are sometimes justified with references to ideology but proponents also often claim they attract corporations whose "skilled" (high-paid employees) desire lower taxes.

● ● ● WHILE THE BUSINESS-FRIENDLY Financial Times may praise a reduction in corporate taxation, the benefits for those of us not connected to the corporate world are less evident. In fact, a reduced tax base usually leads to a decline in spending on important social services like university funding. The effects of a decline in funding are many, but most importantly, at least from a student's perspective, is a reduction in accessibility through rising tuition. Between 1992 and 2002 Canadian undergraduate arts tuition increased by 135%, approximately six times inflation. And between 1992 and 2002 tuition fees for medicine and dentistry increased by 201% and 248% respectively. Today, adjusted for inflation, tuition and incidental fees are at their highest recorded level ever, and more than six times what they were in 1914. Even in Quebec, where a social democratic government and strong student unions have kept tuition relatively low (for residents of the province) the new Liberal provincial government announced that $103 million of what once was bursary funding had been changed to loans, resulting in mass protests in early 2005.

American students have been subjected to a similar assault. At Miami University in Oxford, Ohio, in early 2003 state tuition was doubled. Miami now charges the same for both in and out-of-state students — $16,300 US annually. Similarly, in 2003/04 in-state undergrads at the University of California system began forking over an extra 27%, Arizona State students 40% and University of Virginia attendees 20% more than a year earlier.

"The American Association of State Colleges and Universities, projects that, on average, tuitions at state schools will increase about 12.5% for in-state undergraduates" in 2003/04. This means that the roughly 80% of all American college students who attend state universities will be facing fee increases of nearly five times inflation in addition to an already sizable increase of 9.6% in 2002/03 (WSJ, June 4, 2003).

● ◉ ◈ ONE TACTIC THAT STATE AND UNIVERSITY officials have used to get away with these attacks against students is the old divide-and-conquer routine. Universities increase incoming students' costs but maintain them for those already enrolled, thereby reducing student opposition. It's always a struggle for current students to oppose such increases but we must keep in mind their effects on us personally and the negative consequences for society. We must always strive to keep in mind that we have both individual and collective interests.

● ● ● WHILE GOVERNMENTS HAVE OFF-LOADED tuition costs on to students, poor and working class families' incomes have not kept pace. Families in the bottom quintile of Canadian wealth, for example, would have had to put aside 14% of their after-tax income in 1990/91 to pay the costs of university tuition and fees, but by 1998/99 they would need to devote 23%. Neither have loans and bursary programs kept pace with rising tuition. The Liberal Party's Millennium Scholarship Fund, set up in 1998 to help deal with the rapidly growing problem of student debt, is woefully inadequate. The Canadian Federation of Students estimates that only 8% of the 750,000 students in need of financial assistance every year receive it through that program.

Rising tuition costs combined with stagnating wages and inadequate loans and bursaries are becoming a serious obstacle to post-secondary education, especially for those from poor and working class families. Of the high school graduates who faced barriers to their post-secondary participation, nearly 70% cited finances. Furthermore throughout the 1980s there was no significant difference in post-secondary participation rates between those from the lowest socio-economic status and middle class Canadians. However, throughout the 1990s a gap began to develop. A recent Statistics Canada report found that by 1998 students from families in the highest income group were 2.5 times more likely to attend university than those from the lowest family incomes group. "At the University of Western Ontario, for example, a survey of medi-

The assault on affordable education
continued with the second Bush administration

cal schools found that gross family income of its students had increased from $80,000 a year to $160,000 in the two years since tuition fees doubled to $10,000 in 2000." (Globe and Mail, Sept. 17, 2002)

There is a similar trend in the U.S. According to the Reno Gazette, "The percentage of family income required nationwide for tuition at public colleges and universities has doubled since 1980. The amount of family income that went to pay for tuition at four-year public institutions increased from an average 13 percent in 1980 to 25 percent in 2000."

In addition to increased tuition costs as a percentage of income, loans are dropping. "The average federal Pell Grant award given to financially strapped students going to a public four-year college or university covered 98 percent of tuition in 1986, but only 57 percent in 1999, the report said. State grant aid awards for both low-income and non-need-based students paid 75 percent of tuition in 1986 but only 64 percent in 1999. (5/1/2002) Not surprisingly then "from 1989 to 1999, the average cumulative debt of college and university seniors in the bottom income quartile grew from $7,629 to $12,888 in constant dollars." (www.highereducation.org May 2, 2002) The assault on affordable education continued with the second Bush adminitration in 2005 announcing a further tightening of the Pell Grant system.

⦿ ⦿ ⦿ BASICALLY, POOR AND WORKING CLASS children in North America are being told that unless they have terrific grades or they are willing to incur huge debts, university is not for them. Increasingly students from poor and working class backgrounds are busy working to pay their tuition, so they don't have the time to involve themselves in political activity.

But this is just a small part of the growing class bias of our institutions of "higher" learning. In the battle between various competing visions of society the "one dollar, one vote" reality of the rich and powerful seems to be swamping the "one person, one vote" ideal of the working class and disenfranchised. The neo-liberal agenda has been to reinforce and (where necessary) reassert corporate and elite control over universities. This has been playing out in many ways.

The replacement of government funding with private donations is one of the most obvious ways by which corporations increase their control. There has been an explosion of "naming" schools of medicine and business in return for million dollar donations from wealthy capitalists who have benefited most from tax cuts. While some donors are alumni who truly care about their alma mater, in the majority of cases this money is coming from corporations and others with their own agenda. In Canada, around 20% of university financing now comes from private sources. For example, "in 2000, Canadian universities and teaching hospitals received $161 million from industry for medical research and development, most of it from drug companies. This exceeded the total contribution from all provincial governments combined and was more than half the amount received from federal sources." (Montreal Gazette, Nov. 24, 2002)

In the U.S., public universities are even more reliant on private dollars. Some states are considering completely eliminating state funding.

● ● ● WHERE THIS LEADS is clear. The Wall Street Journal reports that "about one-fourth of university-based medical researchers receive funding from drug companies, ties that sometimes distort study results according to a review done by two researchers with industry connections of their own." (Jan 22, 2003) Similarly, a report by a team of

In their haste for cash, universities are even turning to cigarette companies for funding

Canadian professors concluded that "drug firms compromise research." The National Post says, "The contracts researchers sign with pharmaceutical companies routinely prevent the scientists from disclosing drug risks to patients and the public."

A scary reminder of this was the University of Toronto clinician Nancy Olivieri's now infamous controversy in which Apotex tried to suppress findings that demonstrated the potentially fatal side effects of an Apotex drug. The company abruptly terminated the trials and warned of legal action against Olivieri should she inform her patients at the Hospital for Sick Children of the risks, or publish her findings.

But more generally, the Globe and Mail notes, "Drug testing funded by the pharmaceutical industry is four times more likely to show results favoring the sponsor's product than publicly funded research." (May 30, 2003) So, as the percentage of funding that comes from the drug industry increases, the quality of research declines.

In their haste for cash, universities are even turning to cigarette companies for funding. Tobacco companies benefit from the respectability that comes with associating their name to that of a university. Two years ago, Nottingham University in England accepted 3.8 million pounds ($8 million Cdn.) from British American Tobacco to fund a centre on corporate responsibility (Guardian Weekly, June 5, 2003). Big Tobacco gave Canadian educational institutions $2.4 million between 1996 and 1999. Between 1991 and 2002 tobacco companies gave McGill University alone close to $2 million in gifts and pledges. More disturbing is that a great deal of this money went to faculties of medicine. For instance, Imperial Tobacco provided $568,000 in donations to McGill's affiliated hospitals in 2000 and 2001 (Montreal Gazette, June 17, 2003).

The Globe and Mail nicely summarizes private encroachment

onto campuses during the 1990s: "Financial support for educational programs at universities has grown many different branches over the past ten years. The growth of technology and globalization of education means the dynamic has changed in some instances from a straight-forward donation with no strings attached to a new convoluted partnership where schools now act as commercial interests." (June 4, 2003)

⬤ ⬤ ⬤ ANOTHER FORM THAT the privatization/corporatization process has taken is increasing commercialization under the guise of distance education. According to Forbes, "as the new millennium began, [American] universities earned…$2 billion from long-distance education, delivered through the Internet, videocassettes and other means (Forbes, April 7, 2003)." In his book *Digital Diploma Mills* historian David Noble discusses how the current distance education phenomenon is similar to the (pre-Internet) distance learning movement of the 1920s. Back then, like now, some argued not only the adequacy, but also the actual superiority of correspondence over in-person education models. For Noble, the push for distance education is not a technologically driven movement but rather something being pursued by those motivated by profit and ideology.

The Globe and Mail reported "at the 2003 World Education Market in Lisbon, the majority of exhibitors outlined plans to partner universities and colleges with business through online classes. Already, major universities in the U.S. and Canada have branded their respected name to Internet lesson plans."

A good example of this is Concordia's own eConcordia. It's an Internet venture designed not for educational convenience or social benefit but for profit. eConcordia successfully cuts over-head costs by having one professor teach up to 23 sections where normally they would be teaching only three. Professors can be responsible for as many as 4,000 students at a time! This drastically reduces the quality of education in a university supposedly proud of its low undergrad teacher-to-student ratio. The learning process is damaged when interaction between students and their professors is reduced.

Even the way eConcordia has been set up tells us something about its purpose. eConcordia is extremely secretive. The project is owned by the Concordia Foundation, which gave eConcordia startup capital of a million dollars. The Concordia Foundation is itself a secretive, for-profit company owned by Concordia University. However, unlike the legislated transparency of a public university, only a handful of members of Concordia's board of governors and administration are privy to Concordia Foundation's affairs. The Foundation has repeatedly refused to provide budgetary information to students, who contribute approximately $1 million annually. More than a year after it began operation neither eConcordia's bylaws nor its use of the Concordia name had been approved by the university's highest governing body. In addition, while faculties offer some or parts of courses online, course creation is removed from the hands of the faculty and given to eConcordia administrators.

Of course, another question is what political effect might students taking classes online instead of at a physical campus have on the university? It certainly will keep students apart. If you think this is not part of the thinking that goes into such things consider how far authority has gone in the past to stop student protest. For example in 2003, Myanmar's (Burma) authoritarian regime decided that to pre-empt large scale protest they would simply shutdown all university campuses. They were fearful that large numbers of students together on campus could spark widespread protests against the regime. Some CEOs or emperors with no clothes would prefer the de-politicization of campuses that will result from increases in on-line education. They just don't like us getting together.

CHAPTER EIGHT

AFTER THE REVOLUTION

The best things about the Concordia Student Union student office were the constant debates and the interesting people with whom you could argue. Inside the CSU offices you could find stimulating conversations at noon or midnight. You could listen quietly or participate actively with people from many different parts of the world who voiced opinions ranging from anarcho-feminist to Marxist-Leninist to mainstream social democratic. It was the perfect place to learn about the entire range of "left-wing" points of view.

(The following conversation did not occur and the people named are not real, but the tone, topics and characters are based on actual events filtered through a few years of memory. It is the best I can come up with to capture the essence of what those late night debates were really like.)

"Smashing windows feels exciting when you're pumped full of juvenile male testosterone, but do you really think it's the basis of a political strategy?" said Sam, as he crossed the room to pick up the proof of a leaflet he had just written.

"We need action," said Henri, defending the demonstrators who earlier that day had smashed a few windows along Ste. Catherine Street. "Fight back. The point is to do something that pisses off the capitalists. Smash their property."

"Problem is it doesn't just piss off the capitalists," said Sam. "It pisses off most ordinary people as well."

Henri shrugged.

"You don't care about ordinary people?" said Sam.

"How do you know what ordinary people think?" said Yasir, entering the office along with Simone to the familiar loud 'thunk' of the door closing. "Maybe you're confusing what the media says with what ordinary people think."

"My buddy," said Henri, slapping Yasir on the back. "How was the movie?"

"Good," said Simone, "but kind of depressing."

"Life in Palestine, what do you expect?" said Yasir.

"What are you guys talking about?" said Simone.

"Smashing windows as a form of political protest," said Sam.

"Sam's against it," said Rachel, who had been listening to the conversation for a half an hour without saying a word. "He thinks it's testosterone driven and turns off ordinary people."

"You ever see anyone other than a young male throw a rock or break a window?" said Simone, sharing a "look" with Rachel.

"Young men fight all wars," said Yasir.

"Exactly," said Henri. "It's a war. Class war."

"Gimme a break," said Sam.

"It's part of developing a spirit of resistance," continued Henri. "You sit here up in the ivory tower in intellectual judgment over the people who actually feel strongly enough to act."

"Mindless violence and vandalism undermines our message to the people we want to reach," said Sam. "That's all I'm saying. I'm out there in the street marching to get the attention of millions of ordinary people who should be against the WTO and so-called free trade. If all they see on their TV tonight is guys with bandanas over their faces pushing through plate glass windows and chucking

It wouldn't make the TV news unless some guys in bandanas broke the windows

hunks of cement, that's what they talk about, not the WTO."

"It wouldn't make the TV news unless some guys in bandanas broke the windows," said Yasir. "The media ignores the march unless there's violence."

Even Sam nodded in agreement.

"I agree with Sam about them twisting our message to focus on the violence," said Simone. "It's like they ignore us or make us look like crazed rock-throwing terrorists. How are we supposed to get our message across?"

"You're missing the point of demonstrations," said Henri. "It's to confront power. Show them we're not scared. Get in their face."

"Maybe that's why you're out there marching but most people just want to demonstrate their objection to something or to show the government how many of us are in favor of a position," said Sam.

"Two different, equally valid points of view and that's why we organize two different types of demonstrations," said Yasir. "Ones that focus on direct action and ones that are completely peaceful."

"Except the police use the 'violent' direct action to justify arresting the people on the peaceful marches," said Sam. "A few seconds of window-breaking footage played over and over again goes a long way to justifying a couple of hundred arrests."

"We don't control the corporate media," said Henri. "They're going to make us look bad no matter what we do."

"Sure, but why do we have to make it so easy?" said Sam.

"How do you know it's us breaking the windows?" said Simone. "I never recognize any of them. They just seem to appear and none of them ever get arrested. Why is that?"

"I ..." Rachel tried to say something.

"Agent provocateurs," said Yasir, "working for the cops."

"Right, yet here we are defending them," said Sam, looking at Henri.

"We do something we're called agent provocateurs or we do nothing and we're ignored," Henri responded.

"I …" Rachel had put up her hand, waved it, but everyone ignored her.

"It's not like I'm arguing in favor of pacifism, " said Sam. "I mean it's legitimate to hassle people trying to cross a union picket line or to respond to violence against a community, but I just don't see the point of allowing the media an easy ride on painting us all as mindless vandals."

"I think Rachel would like to speak," said Simone, smiling, but serious. "Gender balance."

Everyone stared at Rachel who looked a little unsure of herself.

"Aren't we missing the point here?" she said. "Violence brings on more violence and who always suffers in the end? Women, children. Where's the line you draw on violence? A little? The state will always respond with more."

"So you are in favor of pacifism?" asked Sam.

"What good has ever come from violence of any sort?" she answered.

"Turn your cheek when they hit you," said Yasir. "Easy to say, but very hard to do when they shoot your brother, bulldoze your home and steal your land."

"Isn't your point that we're all better off if we can keep violence disconnected from politics?" said Simone, looking at Rachel.

"Or is it that those with the most violence will always win the war, so if we know we'll never have as much why would we start one?" said Sam, also looking at Rachel.

She shook her head.

"What?" said Henri.

"Violence scares me," Rachel said.

"Scares most women," said Simone.

"We're hard wired for it," said Yasir. "It's not our fault. Men are born that way."

"Maybe that's why the Iroquois had women run their communities," said Simone. "We sit around and talk, instead of go out and fight."

"Sit around and talk," said Henri. "Maybe that's why there's more and more women lawyers."

"Is that a good or a bad thing?" said Sam.

"They don't like violence and so they get sucked into the law as a way of avoiding conflict," said Henri. "Except the law is just another form of violence used by the rich and powerful to get what they want and keep what they've already stolen."

"You don't think there would be a need for some law even in a classless society?" said Sam, who was taking his leaflet to the copy machine.

"The community can enforce its norms better than lawyers and judges," said Henri.

"And no police to deal with the testosterone-pumped young men out there raping and pillaging?" said Yasir.

"What proportion of their work is defending the existing social order and the private property of a few rich and powerful men?" answered Henri.

"A lot less cops would be needed, I'll grant you that, but there will be a lot of fucked up people for a long time to come," said Yasir. "Cycles of violence and abuse through generations. And we'll need cops to protect ourselves from them for generations."

"If we had real communities those cycles of violence could be broken," said Henri. "You don't need the law, you need grandmothers and aunts and sisters and brothers and neighbors who care."

"A village doesn't produce a criminal, a fucked up nuclear family does?" said Simone.

"Exactly," said Henri.

All societies need rules to protect
the weak from the strong

"How about if you have a fucked up village?" said Yasir. "There's still always going to be disputes between people and kids who are messed up by fetal alcohol syndrome and greed and male testosterone and maybe even a few just plain evil people floating around."

"You don't believe we can make a better world?" said Sam.

"A better village," said Henri. "Concentrate on what we control."

"The question is, will we still need law and cops in our new better village," said Yasir.

"No, the question is why the hell do you need state repression if you have no ruling class to defend?" said Henri.

"I believe in the rule of law," said Rachel.

Her interjection caused people to stop and stare once again. Her voice was so seldom heard.

"And?" said Yasir, after a few moments of silence.

"All societies need rules to protect the weak from the strong," said Rachel.

"More like they do the opposite," said Henri. "You ever watch a cop bash some rich guy over the head with his baton to protect a street person?"

"That would be great if we could send a squad of riot police into the stock exchange to rough up the traders," said Sam. "Or get the beat cops to hassle them like they do the panhandlers. 'Come on, move along, you're bothering the anarchists with your buying and selling.'"

"Not a bad idea," said Yasir.

"Let her finish," said Simone, looking at Rachel.

The room once again focused on Rachel, who seemed uncomfortable at the attention.

"You can't just say we are all going to be equal in everything," Rachel said, slowly, as if she were thinking about each word. "Some of us are more assertive and others scared to speak in public.

You think that will change when we make a better world?"

"You're saying we need rules, we need the rule of law, just like in our meetings where we assign a facilitator to make sure everyone gets a chance to voice their opinion," said Simone.

Rachel nodded.

"Feminism requires the rule of law?" said Sam.

"You deny the existence of anarcho-feminism?" said Henri.

Rachel shrugged. "I know law and the legal system are used to protect the rich and powerful, but that's because the state belongs to them. What if it didn't?"

"Then it wouldn't be a state," said Henri.

"This is an old argument," said Yasir. "Marx versus Bakunin."

"And we know where you stand on that one," said Sam, laughing. "Both of you."

"Let her finish," said Simone.

Once again everyone waited for Rachel to speak.

"All I'm saying is that society, the world, needs a clear set of rules about all sorts of things," she said. "Or people like me get pushed around by those who are stronger and louder."

"And the rules only work if you have someone to enforce them," said Sam, looking at Simone.

"We can have rules without a state and without the cops," said Henri. "Don't we do just fine enforcing the rules about everyone getting a chance to speak?"

"Sometimes," said Simone.

"How about international law?" said Yasir. "What about the rule of law there? What does this stuff with the UN and the Americans and Iraq prove? Those with the most guns will do what they want, break international law when and where they choose, because there's no one more powerful than them to enforce the rules."

"Good point," said Sam.

"We can only end war by achieving the rule of law internationally?" said Simone.

"Exactly," said Yasir.

"The most force must belong to some supra-national body such as the United Nations that exists only to protect the rule of law?" said Sam who was having trouble with the copy machine.

"It's never going to work," said Henri. "Not as long as there are states protecting the interests of their ruling classes. And if there were no states, no ruling classes, there'd be no war and no point in having the United Nations or international law."

"Maybe you're right," said Simone, "but as a transition device until there are no states, why not push for international law to end wars?"

"The Americans would never agree to it," said Henri. "Or the Israelis."

"Maybe not," said Yasir, "but what if the twenty next biggest countries did? What if they agreed to put their military under the command of the UN solely to enforce the rule of law internationally? What would the Americans do then? Fight it or go along with it?"

Suddenly there was a loud clamor as Sam smacked the copy machine. "Shit, shit, shit," he screamed. "This machine is driving me crazy."

Everyone laughed. Simone put her arm around Sam's shoulder in sympathy.

"The revolution will come once we figure out a way of getting the copy machine fixed," said Yasir.

Everyone laughed some more.

CHAPTER NINE

WHAT I LEARNED IN SCHOOL:
PRIVATIZING THE COMMONS

As part of the appeasement of corporate and wealthy donors who were upset by the Netanyahu affair, the BoG people maintained their anti-democratic clampdown on free speech well past the time when even the corporate media thought appropriate.

To protest this we invited Libby Davies and Svend Robinson, two Members of Parliament, as well as Judy Rebick, a prominent Canadian feminist, to speak at Concordia. (Coincidently Libby represents the Vancouver East riding where I'm from and yes I did vote for her.) Concordia's always-agreeable administration decided to pursue a court injunction blocking them from speaking on campus. The admin lawyer argued, without laughing, that it was dangerous to allow these folks to speak on campus "given the inevitable prospect that violence will erupt." Unruly students were bound to get out of hand during the talk. After all, they had the seditious plan to speak about "peace in the Middle East", which two and a half months after the Netanyahu affair was still outlawed at ConU.

Undeterred by a questionable legal ruling, we decided to hold the talk as a form of protest in front of the university's main building. Even though the rally was a last-minute affair (the court decision came down that morning) and it was a cold November day, a couple hundred students showed up to make it a boisterous protest. And once again the national media used this occasion to descend upon Concordia. This time they rightfully ridiculed the ConU admin for its disregard of academic principles, not to mention its disdain of political democracy. The administration clearly felt it had more to gain from its get-tough attitude against free speech than it had to lose. The only reasonable explanation is that the administration expected to get something (donations?) worth more than the ridicule.

At the street meeting Libby made an interesting speech in which she said that the administration's decision to block two members of Parliament from addressing students at a public university was an example of the ubiquitous process of privatizing the commons. While the administration's decision to claim their private rights over Concordia was disconcerting, it was just one example of a much larger pattern, interconnected with corporate globalization, developing at public universities across North America and the world.

Administrators are increasingly running public universities as if they are private corporations. When David Noble came to speak at Concordia he explained that universities "in their own self-conception, are already private. Public universities no longer see themselves as public." In 2002 at York University, Canada's third largest, the university's president Lorna Marsden objected to a freedom of information request by Noble to access York's submission for special Ontario government funding. Marsden said the information should not be publicly released because it contains "commercial information" whose disclosure "would cause harm by prejudicing our [York's] competitive position." According to Noble, this is the language of private corporations. Similarly, in May of 2003 at a meeting of the Montreal Board of Trade, while

It is part of a process of shaping universities in the interests of the private sector

calling on the Quebec government to deregulate tuition, McGill's principal, Heather Munroe-Blum, referred to herself as the CEO of McGill.

● ● ● BUT THESE REMARKS are only the tip of an iceberg. The most extreme manifestation of 'privatizing of the commons' at universities occurred through a change to patent law and shift of focus towards research for business interests. Since the Reagan administration implemented the Bayh-Dole Act in 1980 the process of privatizing publicly funded university research has expanded multifold. This bill allowed universities to patent and profit from inventions discovered with public money. Prior to 1980 research conducted at universities was owned by the U.S. government and was generally held in the public domain. With the Bayh-Dole Act, however, what had belonged to the public became private.

The effects of this change go beyond simply allowing universities to profit from research. It is part of a process of shaping universities in the interests of the private sector. The commercialization of research pushes universities to focus on private profit instead of the public good. It is also intertwined with an ideology that demands an increase in funding for research at a cost to other important roles of a university.

In 2000, universities were granted "3,273 patents; 269 were granted in 1979." Moreover, in 2000, American "universities collected $1.1 billion in royalties from [the] 13,000 patents they hold." (Boston Globe, April 28, 2003) This increase in patent holdings is leading universities to spawn private corporations. According to the Wall Street Journal, "roughly two-thirds of the nation's academic institutions hold stock in start-up companies that sponsor research performed at the same institution." (Jan 22, 2003)

PLAYING LEFT WING

Canadian universities are also rapidly learning how to play the patent game. "In 2001, 27 Canadian universities generated $64.5 million US, an 82-percent increase [in patent royalties] over the previous year." (Toronto Star, May 22, 2003) The perceived benefits of "commercializing" universities are such that "the recent [Canadian] federal budget pledged $225 million a year for more staff and services aimed at bringing research to market." (Toronto Star, April 10, 2003) This, even though commercializing research will realistically only ever add a relatively small portion to university budgets. It does, however, suit capitalist ideology quite nicely: The private market is supreme. The Canadian government's strategy for universities is to direct funding toward what is in the interests of the capitalist market. That is why "the total amount of research funding to universities reached $3.2 billion in 2001 — up one-third from two years earlier." (Ottawa Citizen, April 10, 2003)

Outside of Canada and the U.S. a similar process is being pursued. In 1999, France passed the Allegre law, which, like the Bayh-Dole Act, will increase the patenting of university-based research. It seeks to "create innovative technology companies and transfer public sector-funded research to industry." (Boston Globe) In other words, it emanates from the ideology that claims universities should operate as much as possible in the interests of capitalist enterprise.

● ● ● ANOTHER PART OF THE ORIENTATION of universities towards the needs of capitalism is a decline in funding for areas of study marginally profitable to private interests. This is most clear with the federal government's recent reinvestment into universities through the Canada Research Chairs program, which was set up in 2000 to recruit professors from abroad and to prevent Canadian professors from leaving the country. The Montreal

Gazette writes, "despite the fact that half of all Canadian students are enrolled in the arts or humanities, 80 percent of the program recipients specialize in engineering or nature and health sciences." (Nov 24, 2002)

⊛ ⊛ ⊛ IN ADDITION TO THE SHIFT of academic focus toward research that is profitable and away from other socially useful fields, some "say patents stifle innovation by fostering secrecy among academic peers, instead of promoting an exchange of ideas." (Boston Globe, April 28, 2003) The Canadian Association of University Teachers explains that, "the commercialization of a product depends on patenting it. Patentability, in turn, depends on secrecy. Any public disclosure of a discovery derails the patent process and the new product's ultimate commercialization. From the market perspective, therefore, the tradition of open communication among scholars is a major threat." (September 30, 1999)

Research done collaboratively is usually more efficient. After all, two or a hundred heads are better than one. The research accomplished in the aftermath of the SARS (Severe Acute Respiratory Syndrome) scare, exemplifies the effectiveness of open research. According to Dr. David Heymann, Executive Director, World Health Organization Communicable Diseases programs, "the pace of SARS research has been astounding. Because of an extraordinary collaboration among laboratories from countries around the world, we now know with certainty what causes SARS." (April 16, 2003) In fact, it took less than two weeks to find the mutant coronavirus responsible for SARS. As a result of the scare, research norms were pushed aside and scientists around the world collaborated openly. The World Health Organization in March of 2003 asked 11 laboratories from around the world to participate in a collaborative research project on SARS diagnosis.

Canadian researchers, who knew each other only on a last name basis, from a number of different institutes across the country worked at it together, while in Singapore they created a SARS Clinical Consortium, composed of 15 research institutes. Seth Shulman writing in Technology Review explains; "the success of a global research network in identifying the [SARS] pathogen is an example of the huge payoff that can result when researchers put aside visions of patents and glory for their individual laboratories and let their work behave more like, well, a virus." (Aug. 2003)

● ● ● ONE RESULT OF MONEY being moved to areas that are more conducive to innovation (i.e. private profit) is that students become increasingly neglected. Economically and ideologically, universities are increasingly becoming institutions of research directed towards endeavors of benefit to private interests. David Robinson of the Canadian Association of University Teachers says that, "In the current climate, research is weighted far more highly than teaching is, and it creates a culture where professors are rewarded for bringing in research and corporate funding." (Globe and Mail, October 23, 2002) Students' ability to bring in "corporate funding" is limited. Thus, so is their value to both the academic community and governments. The numbers corroborate David Robinson's fear. "In the decade ending in the 2000/2001 school year, the operating grants collected by universities for every full-time student dropped from $8,607 to $6,991 in constant year-2000 dollars. Over the same stretch of time, federal research grants rose by $455 million a year, to $1.51-billion." (Globe and Mail, Oct. 23, 2002) Governments are choosing research funding over accessibility. American universities have pumped even greater sums into research simultaneous to increasing student costs. "[U.S.] Federal support for basic research in universities has increased

Non-tenured professors are substantially less apt to speak out on politically sensitive issues

from $5 billion to $13 billion during the past 15 years." (Issues in Science and Technology, Summer 2003) While tuition costs are expected to increase by over 12% in 2003, the Dayton Business Journal reports that "universities and other non-profit organizations will increase R&D spending by about 7 percent to $18 billion." (January 3, 2003)

⬤ ⬤ ⬤ ANOTHER RESULT OF DECLINING PUBLIC FUNDING and the ideological shift is that professors' jobs are increasingly precarious. In the U.S., according to the New York Times, 64 percent of faculty members who retired between fall 1997 and fall 1998 left tenured positions, while only 45 percent of those who were hired were given immediate tenure or tenure-track jobs. Now, "some 42 percent of the nation's [U.S.] faculty members are part time." (Aug 4, 2002) The numbers are similar at Concordia.

There are many effects of reduced tenure and increased part-time positions. An obvious one is declining wages. There is, however, also an increased level of insecurity amongst professors, which is harmful to society. Non-tenured professors are substantially less apt to speak out on politically sensitive issues. For example, when I asked a certain political science professor for support in the lead-up to a 2001 Quebec City demonstration against the FTAA, I was told that yes he supported the cause. But he was coming up for tenure and didn't want to jeopardize his position. Non-tenured professors are even more unwilling to speak out about political issues directly connected to the campus, in which administrators have a more concrete interest. This is certainly the case with political causes driven by students or internal faculty issues. And administrators, like most people in positions of authority, prefer that people "who work for them" show the proper level of respect and deference.

Moreover, contrary to the claims of right-wing pundits, this increased precariousness due to one's prospects for tenure is harmful to the social good. Academic freedom, with tenure as one component, was never meant for individual professors. Rather it is intended for the benefit of society as a whole. University professors are supposed to be a source of disinterested information. They are to conduct research and analysis not beholden to any interests — corporate, religious or otherwise — but the social good. Thus they can speak their mind freely and benefit society by coming up with the most truthful information possible. While this has never been reality, it is an ideal worth striving for.

● ● ● ONE MORE ASPECT of the ties that bind universities to the corporate world is debt financing. In August of 2002, Concordia purchased $200-million worth of debenture bonds from financial markets, joining other Canadian universities in a trend that started at the University of Toronto in July of 2001. (Purchasing bonds from the market has long been something American universities have done.) The money was needed to build new buildings to expand enrollment. While the project was (and is) a good one, borrowing directly from private investors is troubling. According to Concordia General Counsel Bram Freedman, "it's private sector mentality." (Concordia University Magazine) Governments should finance infrastructural projects at public universities to minimize the influence of private financiers over academic principles.

The potential power afforded bond holders became real to me the day after the Netanyahu affair when Rector Lowy told me that had the bond purchase not been completed prior to the bad publicity, the new buildings would have been in jeopardy. According to the rector, the events hurt Concordia's investment rating in the eyes of private financiers. If a protest can damage a university's credit rating, then one should also assume that a university's academic moves, such as investment in the business faculty over Fine Arts, or Engineering over Women's Studies, could also improve (or worsen) a university's investment possibilities. Or maybe a crackdown on student protest would improve a university's desirability in the eyes of financiers.

This is not idle speculation. What at first appeared to be tension between Concordia student groups on either side of the Israeli-Palestinian conflict after September 9, 2002 quickly morphed into a battle over the privatization of education. On one side stood Rector Lowy, Concordia's corporate partners and the school's board of governors. On the other side stood the student union, the university senate and much of the faculty.

On October 4, in a landmark decision, Concordia's senate called upon the board of governors to lift the indefinite ban on campus free speech. This vote was in direct opposition to the September 18 resolution made by the BoG to clamp down on student activity. How could the senate and the BoG diverge so widely? Well, the majority of BoG seats are reserved for the "community at large," which, in practice, means members of Montreal's (big) business community. Nineteen out of 23 "community" members, plus the chancellor and two alumni representatives, of the highest decision-making body of the university, were from one community: the corporate world. Other BoG members were:
- five representing students
- six representing faculty
- one representing staff
- one representing the Sir George Williams Alumni Association
- one representing the Loyola Alumni Association (corporate exec)
- one representing the Concordia Alumni Association (corporate exec)

While only 12 of 39 seats on Concordia's Board of Governors are filled with students, staff or faculty, most Senate seats are filled by elected Concordia faculty and students.

This is not unique to Concordia. According to the main student paper at McGill, "the people who make the most important decisions at McGill aren't students or professors, or even administrators. No, the university's highest decision-making body — its board of governors, which sets tuitions fees, hires and fires professors and principals, and constructs and demolishes buildings — is dominated by a Canadian corporate who's who…. the majority of the 45 voting positions are held by 26 'members at large' drawn mainly from the senior management of private-sector corporations. They come from companies with questionable attitude towards academia, companies that donate oodles of money to political parties that would cut (and have cut) billions of dollars from public-education funding." (McGill Daily, October 1, 2001)"

The Concordia BoG has effective control of hiring the rector and vice-rectors. Thus, all of the top administrators are beholden to the BoG, giving it de facto control over all high-level decisions in the university. This control often manifests itself in ways that are harmful to students. For example, Concordia's provost, Jack Lightstone, said this with regards to budget shortfalls to the Montreal Gazette: "universities aren't that committed on how the bill is divided, but someone has to pay the bill." The truth is that this comment represents the administration, not Concordia, since the vast majority of Concordia students would certainly prefer to "divide the bill" with an increase in government funding as opposed to tuition hikes or even corporate funding.

Examples abound of administrators acting in ways that go against the interests of students, staff and faculty. At Concordia these ranged from a vice rector who tried to turn the main area of student space into a corporate cafeteria, to cutting money from services that are popular with students. More fundamental is administrators' role (or lack thereof) in defending public post-secondary education. The leaders of public universities do little to defend the public nature of "their" universities. In the face of the recent assault against public postsecondary education one would assume that administrators, as leaders of these institutions, would be at the forefront in defending them. Instead, this is rare. While students and faculty attempt to defend our institutions from private encroachment, administrators continuously justify (or apologize for) increases in private donations and the general corporate overhaul of campuses.

⊛ ⊛ ⊛ IN OCTOBER 2002, I sat on a panel about public post-secondary education with Concordia's provost, Jack Lightstone. Throughout the discussion he consistently justified the corporate takeover of Concordia. He dismissed concern over drug companies' influence on research. For Lightstone, the Quebec government would always provide the bulk of university funding and therefore universities could never lose their impartiality.

Board members from the corporate world are, of course, more inclined to hire administrators who will run the university as a corporation. And boards have increasingly decided that a semblance of democratic attitude or respect for the autonomy of the academic community is of little importance when hiring administrators. Why should it be any different from what they are used to in the corporate world? Boards often simply bypass the academic community when choosing administrators. Probably the most well known case is Lawrence Summers, a former Clinton administration official, who became president of Harvard in 2001. Not surprisingly, he's been a major proponent of increased corporate participation at that institution. And his comments in early

2005 about biological determinism and women's under-representation in science faculties vividly demonstrates the excess social baggage that comes along with corporate connections.

Of course university boards dominated by corporations are nothing new. Private interests started the first universities and funded them all the way back to feudal times. But, in a democracy, shouldn't we expect our institutions of higher learning to represent more than one narrow sector of interest?

I say it is every student's duty to judge his or her institution based on democratic criteria and, if the rector wears no clothes, let the world know. That is the best way we can pay back our debt to society.

CHAPTER TEN

THE TROUBLE WITH ACTIVISM
— THEY'LL CALL YOU NAMES

While getting involved is often fun, you've got to be prepared to pay a price as well for your activism. This takes many forms, from long, intense hours of work, to being tear-gassed, to becoming the target of slander and lies. (Of course, in some countries the repression can take even more severe forms.)

When you tell the CEO that he is naked, his retinue will most likely respond vigorously. "Guards, get that liar our of here. Slander! He must work for opposing tailors. He's a subversive, a terrorist! He's an enemy of the state, an anarchist, and a communist. He hates the Emperor because he is Swedish. He's a racist. He hates Swedes. Punish the anarchist, communist, subversive, terrorist, lying anti-Swede. He must pay a price for insulting the Emperor!"

What you need to remember is that the more effective your activism, the angrier the defenders of the status quo will be. This includes large sections of the media, many layers of academia (especially those whose job it is to say nice things about the rich and powerful) and most captains of industry. My advice is to listen to their criticisms, ask yourself if there is any validity to it — if there is act on it — and, so long as you are comfortable with what you have done, feel good about the reaction you have provoked.

Was this an assault on free speech?
I don't believe so

When you are playing in the opposing team's rink, angry fans mean you've had a good game.

It's important to develop a thick skin, but it's even more important to know when you're right and admit it when you're wrong. The extreme reaction to the anti-Netanyahu demonstration at Concordia and its aftermath illustrates my point. Protestors were accused by media around the world of being anti-Semitic, enemies of free speech, violent anarchists, Arab terrorists, Nazi-like precursors to the new Kristalnacht and more. Politicians denounced us and corporate donors told the university to get us in line, or else.

All this because of the cancellation of a speech by former prime minister of Israel, Benjamin Netanyahu — a speech to a handpicked audience (people with Arab names didn't get their request for tickets filled), with no question period and to which attendees were told to bring their Israeli flags. Yes, some people who wanted to attend the lecture were called names and a few shoved in the crush of a few thousand people moving about in a confined space. Did demonstrators do anything that I am embarrassed about? That I disagree with? Nothing that I personally saw or heard, but I have been told there were some anti-Semitic slurs shouted. Those I denounce.

As for the "violence" directed at people who were trying to enter the auditorium, an honest, objective, knowledgeable observer would have described it as less threatening than that directed towards people trying to cross a typical Quebec union picket line. Like a picket line, most protestors did aim to stop people from "crossing" into the auditorium and did consider it a victory when the lecture was cancelled. Was this an "assault" on free speech? I don't believe so. Netanyahu had and continues to have many opportunities to have his voice and ideas heard in

Canada. Free speech does not mean you are welcome everywhere. Protests aimed at stopping speeches by people who symbolize an "ism" you strongly disagree with have a long history. Anti-racists have stopped numerous neo-Nazis from speaking at public libraries and other locations in many countries over many decades. Quebec nationalists prevented politicians responsible for the 1970 invocation of the War Measures Act from appearing at certain locations on numerous occasions. People trying to gain support for the emigration of Russian Jews to Israel stopped Alexei Kosygin from delivering speeches in Canada in the early 1970s. And so on.

One can, on the other hand, make a good argument that the tactic of overtly trying to prevent the speech was a mistake because it sidetracked the focus to free speech from the racist, colonial, religious fundamentalist policies that Netanyahu represents. But it seems to me that the over-the-top reaction of the media was, in great part, because the sponsor of the speech was the owner of Canada's largest media empire. And there is no shortage of media voices trying to impress their boss.

As for the charge that the demonstration was a manifestation of anti-Semitism, that the Concordia student union was on the leading edge of a new wave of anti-Semitism I can only shake my head, sadly, at the Big Lie. I know my motivations and I know the stated motivations of many dozens of Concordia student activists. One common theme shared by every one of us is anti-racism and another is a commitment to Canada's official policy of multiculturalism. These, above all other reasons, explain the anti-right-wing-Zionist, anti-Netanyahu, pro-Palestinian fervor among all of us who are not Palestinian. They (a relatively small minority on campus) have their own valid personal reasons. There is an understanding among most student activists, Jews and non-Jews, that discrimination on the grounds of religion or ethnicity is wrong; that all citizens, regardless of religion or ethnicity, should have equal rights; that ethnic or religious-based states are bad; that ethnic cleansing in the name of nationalism is bad; that all colonies must be given independence; that the rule of international law must be upheld. On every count Israel is found lacking.

● ● ● NOT JUST CONCORDIA student activists, but the entire left endured months of vilification. "Israel is the new Jew," read a headline in the National Post. An opinion piece in the Globe and Mail questioned the motives of unions that pass motions criticizing Israel. Zionists on the right and even some on the left claimed antipathy to Israel can only be explained as a revival of anti-Semitism.

Yet left-wing political parties and their supporters around the world have become increasingly vocal in their criticisms of Israel. Does this mean "the left," a historical opponent of racism, has recently become anti-Semitic? My answer is no, with a minor caveat. It is likely that there are individuals who use left-wing opposition to Israel as a cover for their anti-Semitism, but the primary reasons to be "against Zionism" are honestly held, long-standing, anti-racist and progressive.

First, "the left" has always been in favor of secular rather than religious states. Historically, even a majority of left-wing Jews were anti-Zionist for that reason. As a minority population most Jews well understood the dangers of a state religion that required allegiance to be a full participant in the system. In fact, they were frequently victims of Christian intolerance. Left-wing critics of Zionism claim it represents a defeat for the humanist ideal that all people can learn to live together as equal citizens in secular, democratic states. Israel is seen as the modern re-creation of the ghetto.

But the real explanation of the recent growth of anti-Israel sentiment on "the left" is the perception that Israel has become the American imperial attack dog. Anyone who follows world news knows that Israel and the U.S. are close allies and that a "special relationship" has long existed between the two countries. Prior to the 1967 war, the Americans provided Israel with some funds, but since that war, in which Israel proved itself militarily adept, the amount of cash has dramatically increased. For example, at the start of 2003 Israel asked the U.S. for an extra $4 billion in military "aid" to defray the costs of the ongoing Intifada, as well as $8 billion in loan guarantees to help its struggling economy. (Montreal Gazette, Jan 10, 2003)

This is an astonishing sum since the U.S. government only gives approximately $15 billion annually, nearly $3 billion of which, mostly in military aid, already goes to Israel.

According to the Christian Science Monitor, "since 1973, Israel has cost the United States about $1.6 trillion. If divided by today's population, that is more than $5,700 per person." (Dec. 9, 2002) This figure includes direct government aid plus indirect costs such as the increased price of oil. Approximately 50 percent of Israeli debt is secured by the U.S. government, which allows Israel with its massive government debt, to borrow on the world market at a significantly reduced rate. The U.S. has also underwritten much of Israel's domestic armaments industry. This is important, since arms sales provide Israel with half of its manufacturing exports.

In addition, the technology sector, a major part of Israel's economy, is reliant upon government subsidies via military spending so Israel's technology industry is also in effect dependent upon the U.S. Then on top of its financial support, the U.S. has on countless occasions vetoed UN Security Council resolutions denouncing the Israeli occupation of Palestinian territories or other aggressive Israeli actions such as the building of the so-called security barrier.

On the other end, however, we hear little about what the U.S. receives from Israel. Some claim that the special relationship exists because Israel is a democracy. The claim to democracy itself is debatable since millions of Palestinians living under Israeli occupation are not granted voting rights. But, more importantly, anyone who studies history realizes American support for representative government around the world has been haphazard at best. Examples of the U.S. undermining democracy are familiar to those who care to open books and newspapers. In 1973, the same year U.S. military aid to Israel increased, the CIA orchestrated the overthrow of Salvador Allende, Chile's democratically elected president. The 1950s saw an American-sponsored removal of an elected Guatemalan government and in the following decade an elected government in the Dominican Republic met the same fate. Lest someone think this behavior is just ancient history, in April 2002, the Americans funded and consolidated the Venezuelan opposition, which briefly ousted twice democratically elected President Hugo Chavez. More recently the U.S. (with Canadian help) forced Haiti's elected president into exile.

No, the reason for the "special relationship" between Israel and the U.S. is unlikely to be as simple as a commitment to democracy. Some, primarily conspiracy theorists of one sort or another, argue that a powerful "Jewish lobby" explains the relationship. I think that is vastly overstated and sometimes a cover for real anti-Semitism. The rational explanation is that the U.S. funds Israel for military and geo-political motives.

In the 1967 war Israel helped to defeat Egypt President

But those who disagree with this imperialism also must criticize Israel

Nasser's pan-Arabism, which threatened U.S. interests. Over the past few decades, Israel did the dirty work that the U.S. military establishment had a hard time getting by Congress. In the 1980s Israel helped American-backed regimes in Guatemala and El Salvador. Similarly, they funneled weapons to the apartheid-era regime in South Africa.

Those who promote American imperialism may believe Israel is a good and loyal ally. But those who disagree with this imperialism also must criticize Israel. That makes us consistent, not anti-Semitic.

● ● ● FINALLY, CRITICS OF THE ANTI-NETANYAHU protestors have overlooked a few facts. His lecture was only cancelled after police shot tear gas into the building, dispersing a group of students who had occupied the school lobby outside the auditorium where Netanyahu was to speak. The gassing came after protesters had smashed a lobby window, in response to the beatings and arrests of fellow protesters, a scene they were viewing from outside. The student who was manhandled and arrested by the police immediately prior to the window breaking is Jewish. Some of the students outside attempting to help him were Palestinian.

The university administration offered the organizers of the Netanyahu event a number of different locations, all of which were rejected. This begs the question: Did the administration make decisions based upon the desires of event organizers (Asper Foundation) or the interests of students and faculty?

Rector Lowy permitted Netanyahu's lecture to proceed in the downtown Hall Building despite warnings from his own cabinet, security staff and the Montreal police. Many lobbied for the speech to be moved to Loyola Campus, home of a larger venue and a much more conducive atmosphere for the required security. No matter how much one values free speech on campus, there is no justification for upholding it by knowingly endangering the safety of the university community.

Because of this negligence, anyone attending or leaving classes in the Hall Building on September 9 could do so only through a few doorways, as all other entrances and exits were closed off. And when riot police later shot tear gas inside, hundreds of students attempting to evacuate were trapped by barred-off emergency exits and locked doors. This subjected hundreds of students — both those trying to go to class and some protesters — into the forced inhalation of tear gas.

The Concordia administration knew that bringing Netanyahu into the Hall Building was a security threat, which is why they tried to have him speak at the Loyola arena. Instead, they succumbed to outside pressure and decided it was okay to inconvenience students by holding it downtown. This decision should be placed into context. In 2002, Students for Palestinian Human Rights (SPHR) organized a demonstration to be held on university-owned land that was canceled by the administration, for "security" reasons, in the words of Rector Lowy.

CHAPTER ELEVEN

WHAT I LEARNED IN SCHOOL:
HOW TO DEAL WITH THE MEDIA

As I woke up Halloween morning I was excited and nervous and not because of any plans to trick or treat that night. We'd been planning a hemisphere-wide student day of action against the Free Trade Agreement of the Americas (FTAA) for almost a year. Nine months earlier I went with a Quebec delegation to the 2nd World Social Forum in Porto Alegre, Brazil, to spread the word about our plans. We organized a conference with student representatives from all across Canada to coordinate actions and in the month leading up to October 31, 2002, we handed out tens of thousands of fliers, plastered thousands of stickers, put up hundreds of posters, and visited dozens of classrooms to give speeches and take questions.

But that morning I wondered what would be the result of all our hard work. Could we get a few thousand people out on the street — far from the FTAA meetings — to denounce corporate driven globalization? I hoped so, but mainstream news of the planned protest had been scant. No more than a couple of articles, unlike the Summit of the Americas protests in Quebec City, which was front-page news for over a month, even in Montreal. No, this action was truly grassroots so I didn't know what to expect.

As the buses arrived and Montrealers made their way to ConU

Student drug use rising the banner headline read and right underneath it was a picture of the protest

by subway it became clear this would be a successful mobilization. A couple thousand people, as many as I'd hoped for, had arrived even before the scheduled time to begin the march and still the crowd was growing. And then there were the marchers who were assembling at our neighboring university, McGill. By the time the two groups joined together there were ten thousand of us on a spirited and peaceful snake march through downtown streets. I was ecstatic, happier than after any of the successful Halloween candy campaigns of my childhood.

The good feeling lasted until the next morning when I picked up a copy of the only English language daily newspaper in Montreal. What's this? "Student drug use rising" the banner headline read and right under it was a picture from yesterday's successful protest. Student drug use rising? What has that got to do with our march, I thought and then I unfolded the paper to reveal a cutline beneath the photo explaining the picture was of something completely unrelated to student drug use. The editors did it deliberately, I thought, placing the headline and story together to discredit the march. The bastards. Then I wondered if I was being overly sensitive. You're being paranoid, I thought.

Was I? A couple of days later, Hour, one of Montreal's alternative weeklies described the Gazette story placement this way: 'Student drug use rising' is the caption that dominated the Gazette front page on November 1. The adjoining article, which trails inconspicuously down the right-hand column, is dwarfed by a color shot of a gaping protester playing a tambourine. The blurb explaining the photo and the related article sit below the centre fold, allowing a first-glance customer to possibly connect the march more with drug use than with a political demand." (11/14/02)

Was it all an accident? Certainly the Gazette had made its hostility to anti-corporate globalization protestors well known in numerous editorials. According to my father, who has worked as a front-page editor at the Vancouver Sun and coincidently years earlier at the Gazette, that page is looked over, analyzed and discussed much more than any other page in the paper. A variety of different possible article and headline layouts are proposed. Therefore, it seems unlikely that the juxtaposition of the story and headline would not have been noticed and talked about. But, in response to complaints Peter Stockland, the Gazette's editor in chief, played down the connection. "Our [Gazette's] editorial position and the way we play stories are two separate things," he told the Hour.

I have lingering doubts about the veracity of his statement.

⊛ ⊛ ⊛ ONE WAY TO UNDERSTAND THE MEDIA is to read *Manufacturing Consent* by Edward Herman and Noam Chomsky. It is informative to analyze Concordia activists' media experiences through the media propaganda model put forward in that book.

According to the Herman/Chomsky model, the first media filter is the size, ownership, and profit orientation of the mass media. Corporate ownership of the media can — and does — shape editorial and news content. The sheer size, immense owner wealth, concentrated ownership, and profit-seeking imperative of the dominant media corporations could hardly produce any other result. And the ferocious pace of media consolidation that has taken place around the world in the past decade has worsened the situation. Concordia Student Union experiences highlight some of the problems with this media consolidation.

Ownership of the media was probably the most influential reason for the negative media bias we received. By and large the worst treatment came from those outlets owned by CanWest, Canada's biggest media company whose controlling shareholders are well known Israel supporters, the Asper family of Winnipeg. Unfortunately CanWest owns Montreal's only English language daily, a major TV and radio station plus one of the two national newspapers. The Asper Foundation was the external organization that sponsored Netanyahu's attempted speech at Concordia. Nothing like creating then covering the news. While this might sound conspiratorial those who demanded the speech be held on the downtown campus had to have known the response it would elicit.

Israel Asper, the late family patriarch, was inside the lecture hall where Netanyahu was supposed to speak, and was unlikely to have been happy with events that transpired. Presumably, he also did not enjoy the sympathetic media coverage we received after the administration had me arrested and blocked two members of Parliament from speaking on campus. It's a credit to the principled journalists at the Gazette and other CanWest media outlets that we received any fair coverage at all. We were fortunate to have these events transpire not long after CanWest had taken much bad publicity for heavy-handed attempts at overtly shaping editorial content in the newspaper chain. As a result some reporters and editors were in a defiant mood towards their own boss. Fortunately most journalists at CanWest papers and TV stations enjoy some protection through their union contracts.

But of course media moguls always have ways to tell whatever stories they want. Documentary producer Martin Himel came to town with cameras in hand and preconceived propaganda in mind to please his CanWest bosses. His heavy-handed, blatantly one-sided and thus ineffective to anyone but the easily fooled "documentary" called *Confrontation at Concordia* was shown at least three times across Canada on the CanWest-owned Global television network.

Himel, responding to criticism of his fairy tale in two of Canada's biggest newspapers, the Toronto Star and the Globe and Mail, wrote in the Asper-owned National Post that the "tactics used against Jews in Concordia were similar to those used in the initial stages against Jews during the rise of Nazism. (July 15, 2003)" He further elaborated; "Look at the history books or see some of those old newsreels. See how Jews were shoved by cursing mobs, see how thugs broke windows. That's how it all started in the 1920s and '30s in culturally enlightened cities such as Berlin and Munich."

I guess that's why his "documentary" used stereotypically negative images of all protestors, especially ones of Arab ethnic origin. Hillel supporters were universally presented as thoughtful and gentle while the only words from supporters of the Palestinian cause were short clips of anger, taken out of context, usually with eyes bulging. Clearly he felt justified because rather than trying to raise awareness of Israeli colonialism, specifically the current occupation of Palestine, he thinks we are in fact trying to lay the groundwork for the extermination of Jews.

Still Himel went even further with his over-the-top Nazi Holocaust imagery. "If I could get the dust of six million Jewish men, women, and children to talk on this documentary, I wonder what they would say about such placards [at an anti-war demonstration]." This was in reference to the sole probable anti-Semitic image that was actually shown in the documentary — a hand-drawn poster of an evil Israel personified as a man with a big crooked nose — carried by one person in a crowd of 200,000 anti-war protestors more than a half year after the anti-Netanyahu demonstration in an event organized by peace groups, not Concordia students.

To be fair to Himel, he wasn't the only member of the press who either blindly repeated the claims of anti-Palestinian extremists or made up these absurdities. Others also slandered Concordia activists. In the Globe and Mail, columnist Lysianne Gagnon claimed that Concordia is "a campus where walls have been routinely covered with graffiti equating the Star of David with the Nazi swastika." This claim was also made in Himel's *Confrontation at Concordia* but in my three years on campus I have never seen a wall where the Star of David was equated to a swastika (nor did the documentary bother showing us a visual to support its claim). Even NDP MP Svend Robinson, who was supposed to be defending Concordia activists, wrote in the Globe and Mail that anti-Netanyahu protesters threw chairs at Jewish students, which is totally false. According to all first hand accounts and the video footage I have seen, a few chairs were thrown at baton-wielding police, who were charging protestors, no one else.

Still, if a "fact" is in the newspaper or on TV many people, even well meaning ones, believe it to be true. That's one of the reasons why it is important to challenge the lies and biases, even if most of the time it feels like a losing battle. It's also why it's important to support non-commercial, independent media.

● ● ● THIS BRINGS UP THE SECOND FILTER of Chomsky and Herman's propaganda model: advertising. Media outlets must attract and maintain a high proportion of advertising in order to cover the costs of production. Basically all TV and radio (not publicly owned CBC in Canada or BBC in Great Britain or ABC in Australia) and approximately 80% of newspaper revenue comes from advertisers — mostly large corporations.

While it would be hard to find out whether any specific advertiser pressured Montreal media on their Concordia coverage would anyone be shocked to discover that this took place? After the 2001 CSU's politically controversial Uprising handbook was released the Gazette ran an article in which they quoted a company spokesper-

A major function of the mainstream press is to give voice to the opinions of the powerful

son that advertised in the handbook saying I'll "think twice about doing an ad with you [CSU]" next year. So if small-business advertisers consider the political nature of the (relatively inconsequential) CSU handbook when deciding whether to purchase advertising certainly the much more powerful (and class conscious) corporations that advertise in the infinitely more influential Gazette make decisions contingent upon the paper's political leanings. In practice, most probably no corporation needed to call the Gazette. The pro-business philosophy is well internalized within the paper's hierarchy and to a lesser extent amongst its reporters.

⬤ ⬤ ⬤ THE THIRD FILTER listed in *Manufacturing Consent* is what is termed the sourcing of mass media news. The mass media are drawn into a symbiotic relationship with powerful sources of information by economic necessity and reciprocity of interest. A major function of the mainstream press is to give voice to the opinions of the powerful, especially political officials. Perhaps a small part of this is good, since we should know what politicians are doing and thinking. But this filter means that the parameters of debate are set by the rich and powerful who have interests that may or may not be shared by ordinary people.

In part, institutions are given more coverage because the media needs easily accessible stories, which government press conferences and business (or university) PR officials often provide. For instance, Concordia's administration had a whole PR department including a professor who specialized in propaganda (subsequently they've hired a big-time PR firm). Likewise, other anti-CSU groups such as the B'nai Brith, Canadian Jewish Congress and Simon Wiesenthal Centre all have professional media people who sent out press releases or had press conferences denouncing the CSU or Concordia activists in some way. We, on the other hand, had myself as vice president of communications, a vice president of campaigns and some others who helped. Of course we all had other duties aside from our media work and little prior experience.

Still, we did a reasonably good job because we had the moral high ground, youthful energy and our hearts were in the work. If you rely on these you can be successful. For example, I debated the merits of the university gaining a court injunction to block two democratically elected members of Parliament from speaking about "peace in the Middle East" on campus with the professor from the Concordia PR department. During this live noon hour news debate he started off by slanderously claiming the CSU chose the date to overshadow the fall graduation ceremony. It was a ridiculous and untrue claim, but the point of bringing it up was to start me off on the defensive and divert the discussion from the issues where we owned the moral high ground. Luckily I recognized this tactic and didn't bother responding and instead focused on the serious issues we wanted to talk about. The point is, a 23-year-old undergrad in his first TV debate can outfox a media spokesperson schooled in the art of rhetoric if you keep your wits about you and have a good cause. Might, in fact, doesn't always make right.

● ● ● THE FOURTH FILTER is known as flak and enforcers. Herman and Chomsky write, "Negative responses to a media statement or [TV or radio] program. It may take the form of letters, telegrams, phone calls, petitions, lawsuits, speeches and bills before Congress, and other modes of complaint, threat and punitive action." While the Israeli apologist community is well known for its ability to run coordinated and influential "flak" campaigns, the CSU and our allies also did a reasonable job on this front even though we don't have as many powerful allies. The letters section of the Montreal Gazette published numerous pro and anti-letters throughout the year. Often they ran letters that corrected mistaken reports about the CSU.

The power of this filter was brought to my attention in an interesting way during a conversation I had with the McGill Daily features editor just after the Netanyahu affair. I complained to her that the Daily (usually a good student newspaper) owed the CSU an apology after running an article claiming that the "CSU invited Holocaust denier Norman Finkelstein to speak." She said they forgot to write "alleged" Holocaust denier. I argued that while it is certainly true that some right wing Israeli apologists claim he's a Holocaust denier, the charge is actually ridiculous considering that his book, *The Holocaust Industry*, is written in memory of his mother who survived the Warsaw ghetto. To compensate for this grievous error I asked that the features section do an interview with Finkelstein so he could clear the air about these accusations leveled at him. The features editor's response was that she'd do it if Finkelstein was worth it but she wouldn't do it as compensation for a mistake because she didn't want dozens of letters attacking the paper. She never did the interview, which demonstrates that flak can be an especially effective tactic. Nobody likes to get hassled. Perhaps we need to keep that in mind in our relationship with the media.

⊛ ⊛ ⊛ THE FIFTH FILTER mentioned by Chomsky and Herman is anticommunism as a control mechanism. A more apt version of this filter today is antiterrorism and anti-Arab racism. Student activists, and especially Arab men are linked to terrorism. The "mob" is demonized. Even though the students and non-students at the Netanyahu protest included Jews, Palestinians, black people, white men and women, Quebecois, and East Indians, among others, Jonathan Kay still wrote in the National Post: "It is only among the school's Arabs — many of who.... are immigrants from Arab nations where free speech is non-existent and anti-Semitic filth is widespread — that it is considered acceptable to shut your opponent up by force." (If he had even minimal journalistic standards and done some investigation he would have learned that it was white anarchists who led the human chain to block the entry to the building.) The same could be said about the editorial writer at the Montreal Gazette who wrote that the "toxin of mob mentality and tyranny, the corner stone of contemporary Palestinian society, has come to our shores."

● ● ● MOST ACTIVISTS ACCEPT that the corporate media is not supportive of causes which challenge power. There is much discussion about how to direct actions in light of this reality. Some people focus solely on the media side of an action. Others argue the media is against us so let's not focus on them at all. To me the discussion is not black and white: If an action can be "media friendly" then why not? The weakness is not in organizing media centered actions but rather in only doing media style actions. Handing out pamphlets at the bottom of an escalator or putting up posters is not going to draw a lot of media attention, but still needs to be done. In short, the problem is relying on the media at the expense of developing a grassroots base.

Still, the media can be helpful at getting the message out. So, for instance, when we brought David Noble to Concordia to talk about the privatization/commercialization of education this was primarily a popular education event. Not necessarily a media event. Nevertheless, I went out of my way to get reporters from the student newspapers to attend the lecture and report on it. I even wrote an article for the student newspaper (under someone

Like it or not, the media plays a big part in determining people's perception of what you do as an activist

else's name since they only accept one article per author each week) in advance to get the word out and highlight some of the issues he was to talk about. If you can, why not get the media involved? Hopefully the word can be spread to those who couldn't make the event. Similarly, if a demonstration is being organized with the goal of pressuring officials, the media can be a big help to the process.

Like it or not, the media plays a big part in determining people's perception of what you do as an activist. They can be sympathetic or hostile, you can be top spot on the evening news or you can be relegated to a short on the inside back pages. While it's easy to say you shouldn't rely on the "corporate" media to get a message across, if you believe in the power of the people, then you must care about what the most powerful communicators in society are telling the world about you. That's not to say you should make decisions solely or even mainly on how the media might respond — that's a game played in major league arenas, we're just skating on outdoor ice, having fun while honing our skills — but there's some things that can be done to maximize your chances of getting at least fair coverage.

First, those who work for the media come in all sorts of political opinions, biases, backgrounds, work habits and motivations. (I know because my father worked as a reporter and editor of the largest newspaper in Western Canada for most of my life.) Therefore treat each of them as an individual, be friendly and try to build relationships. If you treat them with respect they are more likely to return the favor.

Second, never try to "manipulate" reporters because most of them have very sensitive "bullshit antennas" and will figure out your game all too quickly. While those with power can get away with such tactics, ordinary people cannot. Instead we must appeal to reporters' sense of fairness, impartiality and empathy.

Third, always try to "manipulate" the system to your advantage. This means developing an understanding of how the media works and what is more likely to interest them. For example, get to know the various deadlines for newspapers and TV stations. Television requires good pictures and normally a lot more time, so press conferences earlier in the day are more likely to produce stories that actually make the air. Newspaper reporters can do a lot more by telephone and often can squeeze in late stories, especially when they think it might be a scoop.

Fourth, when you do get screwed by the media (as you inevitably will be) complain professionally. This means pointing out errors of fact, unfair manipulations, biases and other failures in journalistic standards in a forceful but friendly fashion. Complain to the reporter first and then if you are not satisfied, tell her you are going over her head. If a senior editor refuses to take your call, write a reasoned email or letter, with a copy to the reporter. Try your best to avoid interactions when you feel uncontrollable rage. Reason and humor are most often your best tactics. Try not to be a constant pest, because they'll just put you on their "fruitcake" list. If the goal is to pester them, get lots of people involved.

Finally, always have fun. Everybody, including reporters, is more likely to enjoy your company.

CHAPTER TWELVE

A MINI-MANUAL OF CREATIVE ACTIVISM

We need to share information to make the best of our collective experience. Many things happened to us at Concordia that might be interesting and even educational for students and other activists. Problems facing other activists may resemble something that we live through. The following bits and pieces of events and thoughts are offered in the spirit of enhancing our collective wisdom.

● ● ● THE MAIN INGREDIENT in the recipe for political success is energetic commitment to the process of organizing and mobilizing. There is no one formula for bringing about positive social change, but it usually it boils down to effort. However, there are tactics that help. Building alliances is crucial for political success. The activist CSU, in large part, depended on alliances with Arab and Muslim student groups. All too often, these groups and individuals were under attack on campus and a natural alliance developed. Obviously, there must be an ideological component to any alliance but often, when you look for it, some common ground can be found.

Similarly, as much as possible, progressive organizations need to support each other. The relationship between Concordia's People's Potato and the CSU is a good illustration of what I mean.

Events are more social and people enjoy themselves more when food is around

The Potato came into being through a battle over Sodexho-Marriot's (a food company), exclusive contract with the university. Basically, all food on campus had to be bought from this corporation, which had been linked to some questionable practices around the world. Even student bake sales contravened the contract. The student union conducted a campaign that culminated in a "cheese-in" which broke the exclusivity agreement. This led to the establishment of the People's Potato, which serves a free (or pay what you can) four-course vegan meal to hundreds of students every day.

The Potato also became an important mobilizing tool. Because it serves hundreds of meals daily it has an extremely loyal following and many of those people regularly supported the CSU when we needed to mobilize students. For example, on numerous occasions when the CSU organized rallies in opposition to the post-Netanyahu attacks on student rights the Potato served food. Many of those who usually eat at the Potato follow the Potato to the rally. Likewise the Potato crowd tends to be the more politically involved.

The Potato also illustrates another lesson we learned — always try to make food a part of political activities. Events are more social and people enjoy themselves more with food around. Likewise, music adds to political gatherings. A festive political culture helps to draw people and maintains their interest. We want politics to be fun and ultimately we want the society we're trying to create to be fun, as well.

● ● ● SOME PEOPLE ARE SCARED to become activists. Serious students think activism is dangerous to their occupational goals. While no one can be forced to be an activist, we can create an environment where being a good student and a good activist coexist relatively peacefully. This means respecting fellow activists who do what they can with the time they have and not demanding heroic sacrifices. Activism is not a competition to see who can piss off the system the most.

Another point in this regard is that one can learn many important skills while being an activist. Public speaking, writing, media savvy, web development and design are just some of the skills practiced in today's activist community. Political activism has always been a way for people to learn these types of skills. My father learned how to be a journalist through his involvement in anti-apartheid and other activism and my mother's commitment to community health (which ultimately led her back to graduate school) arose through her participation in Latin American solidarity struggles.

The point is to create an activist community where people of many different backgrounds and levels of commitment can come together in a spirit of improving the world. This means integrating activism with their "real" life. Sure, there will be those of us, who for a time at least, become consumed by activism, but if our goal is to create a society that is run from below, then we must understand that many millions of people must participate in their own struggles.

● ● ● CREATING POLITICAL ALLIANCES and interconnecting issues are vital. During the second half of our mandate the attack against Iraq had become the central political issue of the day inside and outside the university. Much of our political energy and thought was directed towards opposing this military aggression. At one point during the semester I attended a meeting of student unions where we discussed a previously planned demonstration for tuition reductions and against the privatization of education.

Both of these issues are critical for students and need to be pursued ruthlessly by student representatives. Nevertheless, while the Bush crew, with quiet Canadian support, was ratcheting up the war rhetoric it was difficult not to fully involve myself in the peace and anti-imperialist movement. A demonstration about tuition seemed of little relative importance. I found myself neglecting the specific directives of my job, which were student issues. Then I realized this was true only if limited to linear thinking. Getting students on the street against the war, in a round-about way, can also advance the fight for accessible education. The truth is, if governments and corporations see students on the street for any issue, see that students are organized and can easily mobilize, they are less likely to raise tuition fees. The process of bringing students onto the streets against war facilitates the fight for accessible education because it politicizes people. It gets them active, which will result in better mobilizations if the government tries to increase tuition fees. Moreover, the anti-war organizing networks facilitate other forms of mobilization. The students against the war network we developed could quickly branch out to fight racism, corporate free trade etc.

The interconnections among political issues and actions are like muscles and nerves in your body. To improve an ailing back one doesn't only stretch and strengthen the back but also strengthens the abdomen and stretches surrounding muscles. Likewise if one wants to improve the education system, it is essential to build broad based support by tapping into existing progressive networks and enhancing others.

The broad interconnection among issues speaks to how a student or labor union should deal with the world around it. Unions, through collective action, should be the instruments that give workers or students a voice when, as individuals, they have little power. Unions should be tools that advance the economic, social

This active student movement is also the reason Quebec has by far the lowest tuition in Canada

and political interests of their members. Unions also need to be involved in shaping the larger political climate, to which they are intimately connected. For example, in Quebec, student unions can be accredited, giving them legal jurisdiction equivalent to a labor union. This is something Quebec's active student movement, which has usually been spearheaded by student unions, fought for and won. This active student movement is also the reason why Quebec has by far the lowest tuition in Canada.

There are connections among Palestinian solidarity activism, the People's Potato and Quebec student union accreditation law. In Quebec, student unions have legal control over how the student positions on university committees are decided, guaranteed dues collection etc. These greater rights give the CSU, as the official voice of students with a guaranteed budget, greater leverage in fighting for student space or opposing racist attacks. We can attempt to raise awareness about the Israeli occupation or take on contracts the university signed with private companies, because we have a certain independence guaranteed by Quebec law. It is much more difficult for the university administration to punish us by taking away our budget or in other ways to interfere, because of Quebec law. This allows the student union to fend off outside groups that are constantly pressuring the ConU administration to weaken the CSU. One result had been that the Rector has called on the Quebec government to de-accredit the CSU or at least weaken accreditation law.

This is another reason to build alliances. In the face of repression, or preferably prior to its development, it is critical to build alliances with mainstream progressive groups such as labor unions or church groups. If we work with and for unions or church groups or international solidarity organizations they get to know us and will be outraged if the police employ repressive tactics against us or the administration tries to expel us from school. We need to be seen as allies and friendly faces so that the powers that be have more trouble dividing and conquering us.

Karameh, which means dignity in Arabic, is a campaign that emanates from the onslaught that took place against Arabs and Palestinian solidarity activism at Concordia post Netanyahu. The attacks became vicious after the Netanyahu speech was cancelled, but they predated those events. In fact, repression against Palestinian solidarity activism has been common for some time. The year before Netanyahu's visit the Concordia administration banned a planned SPHR demonstration, arbitrarily expelled well-known Palestinian activists from the campus and charged SPHR outrageous costs for "security" at their lectures. These attacks led the SPHR to set up a structure to defend itself against administrative repression. The main way in which Karameh does this is through community outreach. Many groups, ranging from the Montreal Muslim Council to an immigrant workers centre, joined the campaign. The community support for Palestinian solidarity activism was there — it simply needed to be tapped into.

In the lead-up and aftermath of the Netanyahu affair, too often the CSU was unsuccessful in efforts to broaden alliances. It wasn't that they weren't available but rather the time we had (felt we had) to nourish them wasn't enough. Energy is finite and we had so much to do at ConU that we neglected much of the outreach. It would have been much better if we had built those connections before we became swamped with attacks.

One group that we did try to build strong links with was the Concordia Part-time Faculty Association. Concordia's part time faculty has been treated poorly by the administration for some time, so there is little love between them. The way the administration handled the events of September 9th became a health and safety issue. Faculty as well as students did not appreciate being tear-gassed and put at risk by lax procedures. We tried to tap into faculty frustration in our campaign for a public inquiry into the Netanyahu affair and our opposition to the anti-student measures taken. We also tried to garner support from numerous labor unions and achieved some success with this.

⬤ ⬤ ⬤ POLITICAL ORGANIZING CAN TAKE MANY FORMS and students have some significant advantages. Concordia is split into two main campuses; one 20 minutes outside of the city center and the other downtown. The Loyola campus is a traditional university campus with a number of old style buildings interspersed with grassy fields. On the other hand, the main artery of the downtown campus, the Hall Building, is just a slab of concrete. Fortunately, however, this slab has a high concentration of students. Approximately 6,000 enter it daily during the fall and winter semesters. Furthermore, almost every one who enters the Hall Building goes up and down the same escalators. So pamphlets can be handed out at the bottom of the escalators to reach thousands. Similarly, display tables in the lobby and mezzanine of the Hall Building can be seen by most who enter. This might be part of the reason why the administration has consistently tried to eliminate these areas as student space. Once before, during a previous left-wing student executive, they attempted to outlaw tables in the lobby, but were defeated with a spontaneous protest. Likewise in the summer prior to Netanyahu they tried to pull a fast one on us by turning the mezzanine into a corporate cafeteria. Both areas, according to the Board of Governors, became a "fire hazard" after the Netanyahu affair.

Having thousands of people crowded together may sometimes be uncomfortable but it facilitates organizing and mobilizing. For example, when I was arrested on October 16th for putting up a table against the FTAA, it was fairly easy the next day to mobi-

Drawing connections between "the struggle" and people's lives helps increase people's interest

lize a couple hundred students to protest. This would have been much more difficult outside of the university setting. A small group of people worked throughout the night to plaster the university with posters. In the morning, they handed out hundreds of simple pamphlets to students on their way to classes. Through the leaflets and word of mouth the news spread quickly. Another reason for the success of the demonstration was due to the slogan chosen for the demonstration. The main slogan was "Help Yves get to his exam." Since this protest was in the middle of mid-term exams the slogan resonated with students, even those not generally politically active. Drawing connections between the "struggle" and people's lives helps increase people's interest.

Making connections with people's lives should always be at the forefront of planning a campaign. People are more open to progressive ideas when they understand the connection between the ideas and their own situation. Further, people are more inclined to be open to radical ideas if they feel that those same radicals and their ideas have had a positive affect in their daily lives. One service that Concordia students associate with left-wing activism is the People's Potato. The student-run pay-what-you-can vegan lunch has been replicated on campuses across Canada. It provides students with an amazing service and for many a sense of community. In addition, it demonstrates that student-run cooperatives can be successful. (The Potato now sells deserts in a number of stores across Montreal and caters.) Many, if not most, people are unwilling to be convinced through ideology alone. They want to taste tangible benefits of the ideology in practice.

● ● ● TAKE ADVANTAGE OF OPPORTUNITIES. As a result of the media attention surrounding my arrest, a space in the corporate media developed to explain my perspective on the matter. I was able to get an opinion piece published on the interconnection between my arrest and the "corporate agenda on campus." I could have reacted solely to the arrest, expressed outrage and blamed the administration and left it at that. But, in the grand scheme of things the arrest itself was of little importance. The bigger picture of the arrest however is important. The connection between the arrest, repression, freedom of expression and the privatization of universities needs to be exposed. Corporate donors prefer universities to be run like corporations. This means they think students should do as they are told. (They think we should all do as we are told.) This means academic independence is at risk. This means tuition will likely shoot up. Activists must help people make connections and present issues in a way that people have not thought about before.

● ● ● PEOPLE NEED 'SAFE' COMMUNAL AREAS to discuss and debate politics free of the boss or the teacher authority. We need space to keep each other updated on events. One important upside of activist control of the CSU was that the student union's space became the central activist hub on campus. Activists came and went at will. As per our commitment to advancing progressive movements in general, community activists were allowed to use the CSU's space. The CSU offices became a communal space to share ideas, plan actions, update each other about the administration's decisions, organize campaigns etc. A radical activist culture permeated the space, which rubbed off on those less politically inclined. Similarly, the activists within our offices pressured the CSU executive into maintaining more principled decisions in the face of pressure from the right-wing media and others.

● ● ● ANY ORGANIZING IS A SUCCESS. During my involvement in organizing a mobilization against the Pacific North West Economic Region in Whistler B.C. I realized that genuine failure is rare. This PNWER demonstration was a catastrophe from the standpoint of size and organizational structure. The rally/demonstration was not well organized and the police were in the mood to make our lives difficult. Nevertheless, the mobilization was better than nothing. In the absence of our protest PNWER would have continued to function outside of public scrutiny. Even with a poorly planned mobilization we were able to at least force the issue into the mainstream press for a minute or two. Anything is better than nothing.

● ● ● THE MOST IMPORTANT THING IS ENERGY when trying to win a student election, just like political activity in general. People have to be willing to make speeches, put up posters, hand out pamphlets, write letters etc... A great idea is nothing without the will to implement it. Usually energy should be directed towards endeavors that provide some type of personal contact with students. The best venue for this is the classroom visit. It combines large numbers with some personal connection. Before classes start professors usually allow for a short presentation on why students should vote for you. Most students already in class will pay attention.

● ● ● IN THE MONTHS AFTER SEPTEMBER 9, 2002, events were chaotic. While we were caught up reacting, it was difficult to understand exactly what was going on. It was tough to gauge our support, especially off campus. Outside perspectives can be helpful. The parents of a few CSU executive members, who had been activists themselves, helped on numerous occasions to put some of the events and coverage into perspective. In large part, the media was against us and it's important to realize that people filter what they read and don't necessarily accept the media's point of view. Support was there, but we did a poor job of tapping into it.

⊛ ⊛ ⊛ POSTERS ARE NOT USUALLY SUFFICIENT to draw people to a demonstration. Neither are pamphlets or emails. However, combined with calling people and word of mouth, these work well. Posters are a good reminder to those who heard about the event through a different outlet. Posters work to draw people to talks and movie nights, events that are a little less engaged. Information pamphlets are especially effective because an issue can be explained even to those who don't attend the demonstration.

In the run-up to the student day of action against the FTAA, we got the word out by giving short presentations to classes on the FTAA, the nature of the demonstration and other events. Even if students didn't attend the demonstration at least they were exposed to the issue. Many students are impressed by the commitment needed to walk into an unknown classroom and speak. Initially it's difficult to get over the stage fright; after a while it becomes enjoyable. It feels good to explain the issues and to take part in making the world a better place.

Stickers can be awesome tools, but they are expensive. We had 30,000 of them printed for the October 31 student day of action against the FTAA and put them up around the city. The best places to put up stickers are on classroom desks or in washrooms for people to read while peeing or being bored by their professors. Off-campus stickers in washrooms, telephone booths, buses etc. can expose thousands to a simple message. Unlike posters, stickers usually stay up for months; the downside is that they must be produced months in advance of any action.

⊛ ⊛ ⊛ THE BEST METHOD of making sure posters stay up is to

use wallpaper paste or wheat paste, which can be made (cheaply) with flour and hot water. Mix until porridge-like.

● ● ● EXPERIENCE HELPS, but enthusiasm, self-confidence and willingness to work are even more important.

● ● ● POLITICAL ACTIONS AND DECISIONS should be public information whenever possible. Secrecy is not our tool. Secrecy is the way illegitimate power/authority functions. Serious long-term social justice is intertwined with the democratizing (political, cultural and economic) of society. Openness is one component of this process since people are more inclined to involve themselves in political organizing that is inviting rather than shrouded in mystery.

● ● ● LET'S NOT FORGET MONEY. Funds are needed to sustain and expand political projects. This is a fact of life. Not paying attention to money does not make it go away. We need to understand this and act accordingly. The CSU played an important role within the Montreal and Concordia activist communities as a resource centre. Thousands of dollars in solidarity donations were handed out for all kinds of wonderful projects, ranging from research to a campaign to halt the deportations of non-status Algerians. One way for activist communities to access funds is by tapping into existing institutions through either getting themselves elected or by asking for solidarity donations. Still, activist projects need to find other ways to be financially viable. SPHR, the main Palestinian group at Concordia, which has expanded to a handful of universities across Canada, started their own printing press. A sympathetic landlord within the community rents SPHR space at a reduced rate. They use it as office space and for their press, which makes some money to further their political projects.

We should not be too self-righteous about which path we choose

● ● ● THERE IS NO ONE CORRECT POLITICAL ANALYSIS. No one even knows for sure that what they believe, let alone whether or not it is the Truth. Analyses and experiences vary. Similarly, there is no one way to effect social change. Some (gasp) may find that they are best able to effect positive social change by working through a political party. Others might feel that labor organizing or being a union representative is what will best benefit society. Likewise some may feel that being a confrontational anarchist activist is the way towards positive social change. There are strong arguments for all three of these routes and many others.

Women might be attracted to feminist organizations. Similarly, people of color often feel they are neglected in a white-dominated activist milieu, preferring to organize separately. These are examples of groups that are faced with a disproportionate share of societal oppression. The lack of recognition for experiences of marginalization is ironic in an activist setting. It is necessary to build alliances and to encourage the existence of spaces in which everyone can feel comfortable.

We should not be too self-righteous about which path we choose. We should involve ourselves in those avenues where we feel most comfortable. Do what you are good at and able to enjoy. People can and should argue for the importance of one choice of struggle over the other, but we should also respect the choice of others. This respect fosters a sense of inclusion and advances the movement. In society as a whole, nine times out of ten there is more that unites us than divides us.

● ● ● ACTIVIST COMMUNITIES often have an odd and self-destructive tendency of excluding others. Too often many committed radical activists seem to differentiate themselves from "normal" people. This may be because of a combination of superiority and inferiority complexes. There is a tendency among activists to see "normal" people as sheep. The "other" is simply blindly following the dictates of the dominant system. While there is some degree of truth in this analysis, it's mostly superficial and elitist. Just because people don't agree with you doesn't mean they are stupid. Maybe they've just never had their mind opened to another way of seeing the world. Don't create barriers to discussion.

Yes, sometimes students' apathy can be frustrating. That is an understandable emotional response. But the point of activism should not be the creation of an elite — that only gets us to places where the system has already taken us.

● ● ● PRODUCING MATERIALS that aren't alienating is important. Too often when creating materials we forget to ponder these questions: Who are we trying to reach? What will catch their attention? How do their visual or terminological experiences differ from our own? If the goal is to introduce or convince those who are not already involved or convinced, then we must find ways to connect/communicate that are accessible and easily understood. Take the art that is used on posters for instance. Commonly the activists who are most committed and have the best analysis produce material that addresses too narrow an audience. Tanks, dark colors and images that come across as dangerous or aggressive are apt to do a poor job at drawing in non-involved people. Instead, simple and visually stimulating art should be used. Text, if possible, ought to be kept to a minimum on posters. This isn't some sort of cop-out or whatever to system. People rightfully fear aggressive or militaristic confrontation. The goal is not to design or demonstrate to other activists our taste in militant art but rather to convince ever-growing numbers of people of radical ideas and, most important, for people to take action (as much as possible in a non-violent manner) based upon those ideas.

By and large people don't want to be involved in endeavors that will be violent, including breaking windows. No matter whether one considers property damage to be violence, we have to accept that for most people (myself included) seeing a broken window is, on some level, offensive. This may or may not be a sentiment that we want to overcome. Nevertheless, if the goal of the action is to empower those who oppose the way in which capitalist globalization hinders human and ecological health and demonstrate the depth of our commitment to the wider public, then offending people by breaking a window may not be the most effective tool to communicate the message. It may actually detract from the message. However, if the point of breaking the window is to do $200 damage to Nike or Royal Bank then, hell, why not. But maybe then it would make more sense as a campaign in and of itself. I don't object to people smashing the windows of big banks with the intent of costing them money. I just can't see myself participating, because I think it would be wasteful.

Ultimately, what we want is the movement for radical social justice to grow. We want people to be convinced of radical analyses that explain the workings of capitalism, imperialism, patriarchy, racism etc. In order for this to be accomplished we have to understand that not everyone is at the same place as ourselves. This doesn't mean that people don't understand the world. Quite the contrary, people usually do. It means that most of the populace has not been exposed to activist culture or even activists outside of media snippets. Many are unaware that we're people just like them. Turning people off who might be convinced that the system is fundamentally immoral and undemocratic simply

It is important for people to feel
that something has been accomplished

because we want to display our militancy, is an error.

We activists can be a thick-headed lot. Most often this is a positive, a stubborn commitment to justice. But there can also be a downside — a stubborn commitment to act in a way that makes sense to us, regardless of the effect on others. Sometimes activists have a short memory. We seem to prefer complaining about the lack of support for our actions instead of realizing the strides we've made. It is imperative that we highlight our advances. Successes need to be savored even if they are not complete — they never will be. It's important for people to feel that something is being accomplished. After all, that's why we struggle.

● ● ● POLITICAL SUCCESS Is strongly connected to waves of energy. Feeling like something is happening helps motivate people who otherwise may be apathetic. Creating global networks can help. Hemispheric-wide days of protest against the FTAA, for instance, were a good idea. Aside from developing an internationalist analysis, the sense of being involved with thousands or even millions of others creates a strong sense of purpose and spurs action. So much of politics is the trajectory of energy. Many people agree that the system is unjust but they simply don't trust that this will ever change. They wonder what the point is of putting energy into it. When people feel that something positive might happen the chance of their getting involved increases substantially. Activists have a crucial role in not only highlighting the many ills of our society but also drawing attention to the positive developments around the world.

● ● ● THE CORPORATE MEDIA is full of articles about the apathy of youth. According to these articles all that young people care about is themselves. Allegedly technologically adept young people care only about consuming. Nevertheless, numerous surveys show that there are more young people involved in community-based organizations than ever before. More and more of us are becoming politically active. There is hope for the future.

● ● ● ALL TOO OFTEN my political activities have been with groups that came together for a certain issue and then more or less disappeared. I've learned that while doing work around individual issues is important it must be expanded into lasting groups or institutions. The work involved in creating an alternative magazine, research group or organizing a union is arduous. Nevertheless, for the movement to expand this work needs to be done. But we should always try to build institutions that reinforce the overall progressive movement. The interconnection between issues is real and so should the interconnection between those combating society's many injustices. Personally, I'm a political animal, addicted to political thought and action. I strongly believe in Albert Camus' statement that to struggle is to live. The struggle itself is central to the political change. Life after all is nothing more than a roundabout adventure.

● ● ● KNOWING YOUR HISTORY might help you survive the slings and arrows that target you when you try to change the world.

Perhaps the most famous student rebellion against racism in Canada was the Concordia computer riot of 1969. Students charged a university professor with racism. A judicial board dismissed their complaints in late January 1969 and they promptly began a sit in. Students occupied one of the top floors of the Hall Building's computer centre, demanding that disciplinary measures be taken against the professor. Students knew the value of the computers to the administration and used that value as a bargaining chip.

On February 11, after a 13-day occupation by more than 75 students, the confrontation climaxed with students and police clashing. The computers were wrecked and the centre was set on fire, destroying student records. This cost the university an estimated $2.5 million (1969 dollars). Students were rounded up and 97 arrested, several served time in jail. Roosevelt Douglas was singled out as the ringleader. He served two years in prison, was labeled a terrorist threat by the Canadian government and was deported in 1975. Was he a bad man? He went on to become the head of state of Dominica, a small island nation in the Caribbean.

The riots prompted Sir George Williams to establish University Regulations on Rights and Responsibilities in 1971, as well as Concordia's later establishment of an Ombuds Office. For the first time students won an institutional mechanism to look at their grievances.

CHAPTER THIRTEEN

WHAT I LEARNED IN SCHOOL:
CLASS RULE AND GENERAL ASSEMBLIES

Do good ideas always win out? Maybe eventually. But sometimes what might seem like a good idea "in principle" threatens certain peoples' perceived interests and they'll fight it regardless of the original good intent.

Picture 700 or so angry students, mostly engineers, packed into a student union general assembly, yelling, heckling, and whistling derisively. One international student, a Mexican woman who speaks in favor of the "progressive" resolution up for debate, is told to "go back to Mexico" (some claim it was "we're not in Mexico") by the angry crowd. The motion is defeated and the testosterone level of the room drops significantly as hundreds of mostly young men walk out leaving the room almost empty.

Now picture 600 determined students from engineering through arts faculties as they crowd a student union general assembly to vote on a resolution in opposition to the planned war against Iraq and systemic racism on campus. More than 95% of those in attendance vote to condemn the military aggression and a strong majority back the call for an inquiry into racism on campus.

Both events happened on the same campus and illustrate an important political point that we ignore at our peril: Self interest matters. Which is another way of saying that some people — particularly the rich and powerful — perceive their "class" interest and act on it.

In the years 1999-2001 the CSU had three successful general assemblies. For one general assembly 700 students packed the hall to demand increased investment in education. On another occasion, hundreds denounced rising administration fees. In 2000 the CSU put forward a motion that called on the Canadian government to uphold United Nations Resolution 242 on Palestine. Even though it angered many pro-Israel students it was successful.

What happened that caused Concordia students to reject the fourth motion? Usually opponents to a general assembly question simply don't show up, which makes a quorum (about 550 at Concordia) difficult. On this occasion, however, opponents did much better than deny a quorum; they took over the meeting. The issue that motivated all these normally politically inactive students to take time out of their day to attend a CSU general assembly was not a fee increase. Nor was it something to do with the Israel/Palestine issue. Stumped? Let's think — what is the fundamental social division within capitalism? If you still don't know, no worries, society goes to great lengths to obfuscate the issue.

• • • PEOPLE'S POLITICAL INTERESTS are many and not always obvious but there is usually some broad interest. Concordia students have numerous "objective" and "perceived" political interests. All of us, to some degree, share student interests, such as quality, accessible education. It's in the interests of the majority of us that the government provides universal health coverage. Of a less "objective" nature are those issues that are more "ideological" or more narrowly focused such as support or opposition to Israeli policy, vegan food at the People's Potato and animal rights.

Then there are the issues that go to the very core of the fundamental division in capitalist society: class. No, not the place where

What benefits one class often is harmful to the other

the prof speaks and you listen. The other kind of class — derived from the way in which we "earn" our living. Or, as Marxists would say: our relationship to the means of production. The crudest way of dividing society is by asking the question: Who "earns" their living by owning the means of production? They are called capitalists. Who "earns" their living by selling their labor? They are called workers. Workers and capitalists are the two great interest groups in society. What benefits one class often is harmful to the other. A wage increase that cuts into the rate of profit is the clearest example of this.

Of course, neither group is entirely homogenous, especially the much larger working class. Different sectors of each class might even have varying interests on specific matters. Capitalists who own automobile factories might prefer socialized medical insurance because it reduces the amount they spend on their employees health cost, while capitalists who own insurance companies will likely think universal government-run healthcare is the worst thing "the damn commies could foist on us." Or the same capitalist may own shares of both insurance and automobile companies. A machinist at an aircraft factory earning $85,000 per year may have a hard time relating to a minimum wage worker at Wal-Mart. Or he (she) might be married to her (him).

Then there are the people whose class interests fall somewhere between the capitalists and the workers. Historically this was called the middle class or the petit bourgeoisie and was comprised primarily of self-employed people such as physicians, lawyers and other small business owners. Some analysts have also argued that there is a coordinating class, which is comprised of people who run the system but don't own significant chunks of capital (money) so aren't really capitalists. Other analysts would include the coordinators in the middle class. The final two classes in traditional Marxist theory were the peasants (small farmers) and the lumpen proletariat (seldom employed workers who subsisted on petty crime, begging or social assistance). People in both groups did not work for wages, so had different fundamental economic interests than the working class.

● ● ● SO, TO GO BACK to that general assembly, what was it that got those (primarily) engineering students riled up that day? On that day, a low-point for student activism at Concordia, 700 students packed a room to roundly denounce a CSU-backed resolution to expel a few corporations from campus for their role in atrocities committed in Colombia and around the world. The motion asked the university to ban Bell Helicopter Textron Canada, Bell Canada and Nortel Networks. BHTC sells Apache military helicopters used to kill people from Israel to Colombia. BCE and Nortel were accused of profiting from paramilitary death-squad hits on Colombian union activists and the U.S. backed Plan Columbia. The companies were involved in the privatization of telephone networks in Colombia, which the workers resisted, fearful for their jobs and other hard-won gains. Yet as the union campaign strengthened, paramilitary forces began murdering some of the union activists, which is disturbingly common in Colombia where some 1,500 union activists have been killed in the past decade. While no one claimed that BCE ordered the murders, they most likely would not have occurred if the privatizations were not being pursued over workers' objections.

The point of the resolution was to make a statement about the Concordia community's connection to Plan Columbia and to raise awareness about the plan. But, the CSU did a poor job at raising awareness about what was going on in Colombia and especially the corporate connections to it. Under the umbrella of the so-called "war on drugs" the U.S has given nearly $1 billion annually since 2000, mostly in military aid, to Colombia. In fact, the plan funds the Colombian state's increasingly intense and repressive 40-year conflict with "leftist" guerillas. The Colombian army has well documented ties to the country's right-wing paramilitaries that murder union activists. (I have to confess a special interest in this, because both my parents have been active in their unions — my mother was vice president of the British Columbia Nurses Union and my father sometimes took time off work to organize for the journalists union. What would my life have been like if my parents happened to be union activists in Colombia instead of Canada? What happens to the children of union activists murdered in Colombia?) Another aspect of Plan Colombia is the repression of indigenous communities as part of the U.S. government's desire to protect Occidental Petroleum's oil pipeline.

But the majority of students present at that general assembly preferred not to think about all this. No one disputed the claims put forward by the CSU about these companies' involvement in Colombian atrocities. Some claimed the corporate links were tenuous, but most who voted against the motion seemed to be uninterested in Colombia. Instead their concern was for the effect the CSU motion might have on their ability to get a job with one of the named corporations. The opposition to the motion coalesced around the idea "how dare the CSU risk our future employment" to make a political point. This spoke to many students in engineering and business who see their interests as connected to the corporate world. Many believe that what benefits corporations will (eventually) be good for them. Of course, things may not work out the way they have planned. Later in life these engineering or business students may very well change their minds and decide they are more workers than owners.

The thought that we might insult a few companies motivated some engineering students to organize their faculty. (Two years later one would become CSU president as part of a right-wing backlash coordinated with thousands of dollars of outside help.) They, along with faculty and the administration, were able to mobilize students quite effectively. The dean of engineering and computer science sent at least two emails to all professors in his department telling them to encourage students to participate in the general assembly and to spring them from class. The administration did not afford this same luxury to those in social sciences and fine arts, the sphere of study where students tend to be more socially aware and critical of the prevailing system.

● ● ● STILL, THE CSU WAS ABLE to overcome administration interference on other occasions. One reason for this is something that makes the Concordia political scene unique. A large percentage of engineering students (and some business students), who at most universities would either not vote or vote for the apolitical (right-wing) student representatives, at Concordia vote for left-wing, activist candidates for the CSU. Arab-Canadian engineering students make up a sizable chunk of the left's supporters. (There are up to 5,000 Arabs out of a total university population of 30,000 students.) Because of the work of groups such as the Students for Palestinian Human Rights and the Muslim Students Association many feel compelled to involve themselves in student politics or at least support those who are defending their community.

While many of these students feel the brunt of campus racism and support Palestinian rights, they are engineering or business students who often see their interests intertwined with those of corporate capitalism. So, when forced to choose between supporting the CSU or their (perceived) class interests they abandoned

They were engineering and business students of many backgrounds who shared a common class interest

their allies on the left. Some actively campaigned against the CSU.

This is not to say that Arab-Canadian engineering students were the sole cause of the resolution's defeat. The majority of those at the general assembly were not Arab-Canadians. They were engineering and business students of many backgrounds who shared a common class interest. But the loss of support from the Arab-Canadian engineering students was a key blow, which a few weeks later resulted in a recalled CSU executive.

So, the difference between this resolution and other later ones that were successful was that the later ones could easily be supported by all of the CSU's core constituencies: Anarchist activists oppose racism and war; Arab students oppose the attack against Iraq and obviously the racism directed at them. Less politicized students could relatively easily support the anti-war motion and while they may not have attended just for the racism question they certainly didn't oppose it.

● ● ● THE LESSON IS that university students generally have a certain level of privilege. Attending university is expensive both in tuition costs and foregone wages. Likewise, not everyone has the prior educational opportunities needed to attend. Most people attending university will end up as part of the working class but a significant number are at least dreaming of the middle or ruling class.

When activists complain that the reason more people haven't joined the movement is that people only care about their own self-interest, it is only partly true. From the standpoint of an organizer, self-interest can be a bad thing because it is associated with people just going about their personal business with little concern for the rest of the world, especially for those who take on the brunt of Western imperialism. On the other hand, self-interest can be a powerful tool for activists because the vast majority of the world is (or is becoming) working class. One day the majority of us may realize it's in our self-interest to redesign our economy so that it is run on the principle of one person, one vote instead of the current one dollar, one vote. Ultimately, the world will only change when a large enough group of people perceives it to be in their self-interest to change it. People in common cause need to take control of our communities, culture and workplaces; restructure them so they function in our collective self-interest.

This phenomenon of self-interest in the context of encroaching corporate interests on campus also brings up what can sometimes be a difficult question for activist student unions. When we challenge and even defeat specific corporate interests involved on our campuses there can be negative repercussions. As a student union, the CSU had to juggle the question of the long-term interests of society and the (perceived at least) short-term interests of many of our members, current students. Where does the CSU draw the line between what we consider to be a positive ideal — the struggle against corporate involvement on campuses, especially corporations with dubious human rights records — and potential jobs for students and money for the university?

Students unions, not to mention labor unions, working within the capitalist system, have to deal with these types of contradictions every day. Often, it's easy for outside activists to criticize unions for their lack of activist/radical nature. But, unlike students, most workers will be stuck as workers for a long, long time. They don't graduate. So, workers and union activists inevitably come up with some sort of accommodation with their bosses. It's necessary to survive.

But the very temporary nature of being a student is what gives us a special privilege and responsibility. We don't necessarily have to accommodate ourselves to the power of the university administration, because we will soon be gone. While we do need to concern ourselves with the day-to-day representation of the students we represent, we can more easily take on wider societal questions. We can more easily be the conscience of our society. What's the worst thing the university administration can do to us? Suspend us? Expel us? They can and they did to me and it's not so bad. They suspended me for one semester and then another because I stepped foot on campus to fulfill my duties as a CSU council member. Then I was expelled for five years because I was re-elected to council and tried to take my seat at a meeting, which was once again held on campus. Once again a dozen cops showed up to drag me away. As I write this, my appeal is winding its way through the courts. Regardless of what happens I have few regrets. I have had fun and learned a lot. What more can one ask from school?

And even though the left wing slate lost control of the CSU executive after our year of confrontations, we still won a majority of seats on council. More important we stood up for what we believed. We questioned authority. Doing so doesn't mean you will win all your battles. In fact, you will undoubtedly lose more often than not. But while winning is great, as many of my hockey coaches said, it matters more how you play the game. We have a responsibility and privilege as students to voice awkward questions, even the ones that make some of our fellow students angry.

Those damn activists! Always caus-
ing trouble. Disrupting our peace and quiet. What's all
this have to do with getting an education, anyway? Leave me
alone to attend classes and do my homework. I just want to go to
school and not see these damn troublemakers every day!

It's no surprise that many people, both on and off campuses
around the world, feel this way. Most of us want to do well at
school, earn decent marks and get on with our lives. Or do our
jobs and go home. Sometimes, activism can seem like a lot of
sound and fury signifying nothing. People have said to me: "Sure I
agree that peace and justice in the Middle East is a good idea, but
what's the point of demonstrating — nothing ever changes." Or,
"Of course the world would be a better place if everyone had clean
drinking water and proper sewage systems, but there's nothing I
can do about it." Or, "Yes, corporations have too much power, but
do you think they care if a few thousand people march in the
street?" Or, "Things are the way they are and that's how it is and
always will be. All your complaining and noise will do nothing to
change anything."

One problem with these arguments is that democracy requires
active citizens. If politics becomes the exclusive domain of professional politicians and lobbyists, we might as well invite history's

dictators back to rule in the name of efficiency and getting the trains to run on time. Another response to these objections/excuses about activism is to imagine what the world would be like without activists. From my reading of history, we could move back in time this way:

Women would be stuck at home raising babies or have an extremely narrow range of job choices if there had been no women's liberation activism in the past few decades. There'd be no daycare, a husband striking a wife would still be legal and abortions would be illegal in all circumstances.

Homosexuality would be illegal, without the gay rights movement of the past few decades.

Without the environmental activists of the last forty years, there'd be no clean air or clean water legislation, no ban on harmful pesticides, no preservation of species acts, no limits to fishing methods, no restrictions on logging, a lot fewer parks, a lot more nuclear power plants, a lot more dirty coal-fired power plants, a lot more dams, less efficient car engines, less efficient refrigerators and washing machines and an even bigger hole in the earth's ozone layer.

Without the world-wide struggle to end apartheid from the 1950s to the 1990s, and especially the courageous activism of South Africans themselves, the white minority would still be in power.

If there had not been civil rights activists from the 1920s until today, there would still be segregation in the United States, Asians would not be able to vote in Canada or other white settler states and native peoples throughout the Americas and other continents would not have even minimal citizenship rights.

If there had been no anti-war activists in the 1960s and 70s, Vietnam may not have united.

Without the suffragette activists women would not have the right to vote

If there had been no worldwide demonstrations of support for Solidarnosc in Poland, Socialism with a Human Face in Czechoslovakia and the Hungarian Uprising, it would have been much easier for the Russian troops to remain throughout Eastern Europe.

Without the millions of anti-colonial activists from the 1920s to the 1970s, Africa, the Caribbean and most of Asia would still "belong" to European powers.

Without the suffragette activists from the late 1800s well into this century, women would not have the right to vote.

Without millions of union activists around the world over the past 150 years, there would be no limits on the working day, children everywhere would still work instead of attend school, there'd be no public or private pensions, no unemployment insurance, no disability insurance, no health and safety legislation, no workers' compensation, no minimum wage, no vacation pay, no statutory holiday pay, no equal pay for work of equal value, no grievance procedure, no overtime, a lot poorer wages and unlimited management rights.

Without the labor activists who worked with millions of social activists over the past 150 years, there'd be no vote for anyone except for a privileged few white men, no public school system, no public universities, no retirement legislation or social security, no public healthcare systems, no right to join a union, no welfare systems, no public health systems, a lot poorer sewage and potable water systems, no graduated income tax, no income tax and no social programs of any kind.

Without the anti-slavery activists of the 1800s there would still be millions of people bought and sold, then transported against their will to distant parts of the world where they would often be worked to death.

● ● ● ONE OF THE VERY BEST EXAMPLES of what can be accomplished by organized and dedicated student activists is the Berkeley Free Speech movement. In 1934 the president of the University of California at Berkeley banned all political and religious activity from the campus. On numerous occasions over the years students attempted to overturn the ban but a concerted campaign didn't materialize until 1964 when the university administration declared a stretch of Telegraph Avenue, the Bancroft strip, just outside the main gate to the Berkeley campus, off limits for political activity. The area had become associated with demonstrations against Berkeley and Oakland businesses that practised discrimination. The conservative university regents pressured Berkeley to close this recruiting ground for activists and restrict student agitation in adjacent areas.

The free speech controversy then exploded from registration week in September through December 10th, 1964. An alliance of student groups including socialist groups, religious organizations, civil rights groups, the Young Democrats and Young Republicans came together. According to a graduate student report, "The original rule changes desired by the students fall into four categories. They opposed the university ban on fund-raising and selling literature... the ban on recruiting members on campus and holding membership meetings... They asked the university to rescind rules which 'harassed' the flow of ideas: the rule requiring 72-hour notification if an off-campus speaker is to speak on campus, the rule requiring a tenured faculty member to moderate all political and all 'controversial' meetings; and the practice of billing groups for police protection if the university decided it wanted policemen at the meeting... The students regarded the ban on 'advocacy' as a direct infringement of their Constitutional guarantees of free speech. They opposed any restriction on advocacy, but the details of the student position took different forms as the administration changed its position." (www.fsm-a.org) After the suspension of eight prominent activists, students added a demand for the university's police and judicial powers to be separated so that instead of the chancellor having control over disciplinary matters the faculty be given jurisdiction in disputes arising over the rules on political activity.

After some 800 people were arrested in a peaceful sit-in the events reached the point where on Friday December 4, 8,000 students attended a Free Speech Movement afternoon rally. "[A] strike on December 3-4 was supported by 60 to 70 percent of the [27,000-strong] student body" and most teachers assistants and even faculty supported it. On December 8 the academic senate voted 824-115 in favor of the substantive demands of the FSM and by January the regents had more or less given in to student demands.

● ● ● IT'S INTERESTING TO LEARN that students back in the 1960s were fighting some of the very same battles that we faced at Concordia in the 21st century. The university administration often arbitrarily adds extra security, especially for Solidarity for Palestinian Human Rights and Muslim Students Association events, and passes the prohibitive costs on to the student groups. The room bookings department and security regularly delay authorization for political events. It was Concordia's equivalent to the regents, the BoG, that banned student activities, political or otherwise, in the major areas of the university in the aftermath of the Netanyahu protest. And the battle to maintain the division of police and judicial powers, to stop Concordia's Rector from being judge, jury and executioner, continues. It seems no matter where in the world students take action, especially if successful, we are faced with similar battles to limit our ability to freely express and organize ourselves.

Students also played a major role in the U.S. civil rights movement of the 1950s and 60s. Students in France in 1968 joined with unions and other organizations bringing millions of people into the street to successfully demand major societal change. In the same year Czech students and others confronted tanks in what seemed at the time like a major defeat for democracy, but which in hindsight is seen as a critical event ultimately leading to the dismantling of the Russian empire in Eastern Europe. Students also played a key role in demanding democracy in Latin America, Burma, Korea, China, Pakistan and throughout Africa.

This is by no means a comprehensive list, but the message is clear: Activism works. Without people willing to put in time and effort, sometimes even risking their lives to confront the system, the world would be a much worse place for the vast majority of humanity. Throughout every age, going back to the beginning of human thought, some people (usually the richest and most powerful) claimed that the way things were was the very best civilization could ever offer. Other people dreamed of improving the world and of doing things a different way. The two sides have always clashed and out of that confrontation has come change and progress.

Through the ages activism has required people who are willing to dream, to discuss and to act. Those who have done this have given humanity so much. To me, activism seems the least we can do for our future.

So student activism can "confront" authority and undermine the system — so what, many people might say. Have they got a better idea? A better system? What's the alternative? Strengthened controls on international finance and an improved immigration system might be good. Increased funding for public health promotion is probably necessary. Free education, small classes and student control over our campus and curriculum are agreeable to some. You might tinker with the system, making changes here and there but capitalism is here to stay.

Of course, a long time ago people said the same thing about the Roman Empire, feudalism and slavery, but they all disappeared. Many people believe there is no realistic alternative to capitalism, but I do. Millions of others believe and have believed that another system is not only possible, but necessary — maybe even inevitable. Over the past two centuries alternatives have been written about and discussed, political parties have been created, wars have been fought, institutions created and experiments tried. While most of us under 30 years old have had little or no contact with these alternative ideas, they do exist and are certainly a good place to start in building a better world.

We need to read about, debate and try out the ideas for ourselves. In this spirit a brief summary of some of the main historic alternatives to capitalism follows.

⊛ ⊛ ⊛ SOCIAL DEMOCRACY — Social democratic movements and political parties have been by far the most successful of all the anti-capitalist currents in the last 150 years, even if many would argue that they strengthen, rather than weaken the existing system. People inspired by social democracy were instrumental in winning almost every important reform in countries around the world. These include: universal suffrage, pensions, unemployment insurance, universal healthcare, public education, union rights, minimum wage, human rights protection and workers compensation.

Social democracy was founded as a Marxist movement under the banner of the Second International (the First International was essentially an attempt to create a world-wide union movement) in 1889. In many European countries the movement quickly achieved significant electoral success and by the outbreak of the First World War in 1914 Second International affiliated political parties had many members sitting in national parliaments throughout Europe. Despite their claimed internationalism, most of these social democratic politicians placed themselves on the side of their respective "fatherlands" and supported the war, which resulted in the slaughter of millions through 1918. This failure to oppose a capitalist war alienated some within their organizations and in 1917 the Second International was further divided over support for the Bolshevik Revolution in Russia. A short while later one faction split off to found the Third International, a world-wide network of self-proclaimed communist parties that supported the Soviet Union. Despite (perhaps even because of) the split, by the 1930s social democratic parties achieved the status of government in countries as diverse as Sweden and New Zealand. By the 1970s social democracy arguably had became the dominant ideology in much of Western Europe.

Within social democracy there were and are, broadly, two strains: Those who support capitalism, but with strong labor regulation, social services, environmental protections, nationalized industries, economic protectionism etc. and those who see social democracy as the gradual replacement of capitalism with a more humane economy and society. Of course the "capitalism with a human face" strain has been the dominant one, especially in countries where the parties have long governed.

The most significant limitation to this strain of thought is that so long as there are concentrated sources of capitalist power (corporations) there will be a push for more unregulated forms of capitalism no matter how socially destructive. Likewise, poverty, even in the most advanced social democratic countries such as Sweden, has not been completely eradicated. In addition, social democratic political parties have been all too willing to join their countries' imperial adventures. In fact, supposedly social democratic governments have been at the forefront of imperial adventures — witness Tony Blair's Labor government and its "coalition of the willing" with the USA in Iraq.

● ● ● MARXISM-LENINISM — The second most successful strain of anti-capitalist thought has been Marxism-Leninism. People inspired by these ideas have taken state power (became the government) in numerous countries, including Russia, China, Vietnam and Cuba. Vladimir Lenin, a Russian revolutionary who was a member of the Second International, built a political party with a strict hierarchical structure to confront the severe state

The idea of a tightly-knit professional party that could overcome severe repression was attractive

repression in his country. The Bolsheviks (this means "majority" in Russian and refers to an internal split in that country's Social Democratic Party) were successful, in the midst of the First World War, in organizing within the small working class and especially in the disintegrating military. They managed to militarily overthrow the existing government and then fight a lengthy civil war to eventually create the Soviet Union.

The essential Leninist idea is that the "most advanced" socialists come together in a tight-knit, professional political party that can be the "vanguard" of the working class, taking state power in its name. This party is then supposed to eventually build a communist system wherein there are no classes and the principle of "from each according to their ability, to each according to their need" reigns supreme.

The success of the Bolsheviks in Russia caused many social democratic activists around the world to create communist parties and join the Third International. The idea of a tightly-knit professional party that could overcome severe repression was attractive. Communist parties around the world grew rapidly, especially in the midst of the Great Depression of the 1930s.

Very quickly however, different strains of Marxism-Leninism developed. The first was Trotskyism. Leon Trotsky was an on-again, off-again Bolshevik who eventually became the leader of the Red Army fighting the enemies of the revolution in the Russian civil war. After Lenin's death less than a decade after the 1917 revolution, Trotsky lost a power struggle with the head of the Bolshevik secret police, Joseph Stalin, and was forced into exile. The main point of theoretical disagreement between Trotsky and Stalin was over "socialism in one country." Trotsky argued that socialism could only be built in the advanced capitalist countries of Western Europe and North America and that the role of the communist parties must be to push for "permanent revolution" until capitalist power was destroyed around the world. Stalin, as head of state argued that socialism could be built in Russia and that a critical role of communist parties around the world was to defend the Soviet Union. From the 1930s until the 1960s Trotskyism (Trotsky was murdered by an agent of Stalin in 1940), organized as the Fourth International, was a sort of Marxist-Leninist counter-culture to the official communist parties.

The next major Marxist-Leninist current was Maoism, which for a while was the official ideology of China. Mao Tse-tung was the leader of the Chinese Communist Party, which fought a successful decade and half long war to achieve state power in 1949 and re-unify a country that had been divided up into spheres of influence by European and then Japanese imperialists. The unique features of Maoism were a strong current of nationalism, an emphasis on the peasant class, guerrilla warfare and a claim to be inheritors of the "correct" (Stalinist) communist legacy after the death and then renunciation of Stalin by the Soviet leadership in the late 1950s. Maoism enjoyed a brief period of popularity among students and intellectuals in many parts of the world in the late 1960s and early 1970s. For example, many former student activists in the USA, Europe and Canada organized small political parties that claimed to be based on Maoism.

The other significant strain of Marxism-Leninism was based on the thoughts and activities of Che Guevara and the Cuban revolution that achieved power in 1960. The focus was on the creation of a small guerrilla army that could gradually grow and take state power through armed struggle. Many Latin American students were attracted to these ideas in the 1960s and 70s. U.S.-backed military governments crushed most of these armed struggles.

An important criticism of Marxism-Leninism is that it seems

to be more the ideology of an army achieving state power, rather than the working class or the people. A political party ruling in the name of the working class or the people is not the same thing as the working class or all the people ruling themselves. One result was mass repression and the death of millions of people, all in the name of communism. While Marxist-Leninist governments achieved some good things, I am unaware of any that have actually built a real democratic society where the economy and social structure is run by and for ordinary people.

❋ ❋ ❋ ANARCHISM — Anarchism has its roots in a nineteenth century split between Mikhail Bakunin and Karl Marx. The central disagreement was over the role of the state (government). While Marx argued for taking over the state and using it to transform and abolish capitalism, Bakunin's position was that the state must be abolished. The country where anarchism achieved its greatest success, in terms of influence, was Spain in the 1930s. Before and during the Spanish Civil War (1936-39) anarchist collectives self-administered much of the economy.

There have been a variety of different left anarchist (socialist libertarian) strains of thought ranging from primitivism to syndicalism. What all anarchists agree upon, however, is a negative. According to the *American Heritage College Dictionary*, anarchism is "the doctrine that all forms of government are unnecessary, oppressive, and undesirable and should be abolished." When thinking about anarchism it's important to differentiate between society and government since anarchism is not necessarily antagonistic to society.

❋ ❋ ❋ ANARCHO-COMMUNISM/LIBERTARIAN-SOCIALISM — Anarcho-communism/libertarian-socialism is summed up in the name: adherents believe that management of the common good (socialism) is necessary, but that this should be done in a manner that preserves individual liberty and avoids concentration of power or authority (libertarianism). Some libertarian socialists say individual liberty and societal harmony are necessarily antagonistic and that anarchist philosophy must balance the two. Others feel that the two are symbiotic and that the liberty of the individual guarantees the harmony of the society and vice-versa.

All the critiques that anarchists develop are based on principles of decentralization of power and authority. So, while anarchists have a critique of capitalism similar to Marxism, the basis for opposition to capitalism is that it leads to concentration of power (in the form of wealth). This critique highlights the distinction between libertarian socialists and Libertarians: Libertarian socialists advocate freedom while denying, to a greater or lesser extent, the legitimacy of private property, since private property in the form of capital leads to the exploitation of others with lesser economic power and thus infringes on the exploited class' individual freedoms. Libertarians, by contrast, believe that liberty is impossible without the enforced protection of private property.

In lieu of states, libertarian socialists seek to organize themselves into voluntary institutions (usually called collectives or syndicates) that use direct democracy or consensus for their decision-making process. Most libertarian socialists do not consider themselves utopian and try to avoid predictions of what a future society would or should look like. The tradition instead has been that such decisions cannot be made now and must be made through struggle and experimentation.

The historic weakness of libertarian socialism, in my opinion, has been its denial of any utility for the role of the state in

The values underpinning Parecon are solidarity, diversity, equity and self-management

making life better for ordinary people. Ironically, in some ways this position corresponds with that of neo-liberals and so-called Libertarians.

◉ ◉ ◉ PARTICIPATORY ECONOMICS (PARECON) — As noted above, the anarchist tradition has been one of avoiding predicting what a future society should look like, but parecon, originally set out by both Robin Hahnel and Michael Albert, though pushed more forcefully in recent years by Albert — a founder of South End Press and Z magazine and current editor of Znet (zmag.org) — is an elaborate alternative that has garnered some attention. The values underpinning parecon are solidarity, diversity, equity, and self-management. Albert's project is to seek "new institutions that further rather than subvert our preferred values."

This is accomplished by:

"First, in any parecon we have worker and consumer councils. We have said that we are going to have self-management of economic decisions and, if that is the case, then economic actors will of course need a place to express their preferences — and even to develop them — so they can proportionately influence outcomes. This occurs in the councils, which vary in size from individuals, living units, and neighborhoods, to regions and countries, and from work teams, divisions, and workplaces, to industries and whole economies. Within the workers and consumers councils communication and decision making occurs by different means in different cases and contexts, but the overriding principle is always that the means chosen should apportion decision-making say to actors proportionate to the impact of outcomes on those actors.

"Second, in a parecon we have balanced job complexes to replace the corporate division of labor that we now endure. In any economy, we take all the tasks in a workplace and combine some into one job, some into another, and so on. The change from capitalism to a participatory economy is that in a parecon we choose a mix of tasks for each job such that every job has an empowerment effect and a quality of life effect like every other job — a balanced job complex.

"You do a job and so do I. We don't do the same things, most likely. People have different jobs in different workplaces and in each workplace, both to get things done sensibly and because we have different tastes, talents, and preferences. But the mix of tasks that you do composing your job has the same overall quality of life and empowerment 'rating' as the mix of tasks I do composing my job. There is no longer a class of actors who monopolize empowering conditions and circumstances — I call these the coordinator class — while another class of actors (workers) does only rote, tedious, or otherwise un-empowering work.

"There is still surgery, but those who do it do other balancing tasks as well — perhaps cleaning bedpans. There is still answering phones and working in mines, but those who do it do other tasks as well, either in their main workplace or elsewhere — with the total that everyone does balancing out regarding empowerment and quality of life implications.

"In other words, parecon not only eliminates capitalists as a class (by eliminating private ownership of productive property), it also eliminates coordinators as a class (by eliminating monopolization of empowering circumstances). In a parecon we are all workers with balanced job complexes — there is one class, only.

"Third, in a parecon we remunerate workers for effort and sacrifice only. Those who can't work of course receive their income by right, an innovation that even social democracy and variants of capitalism respect. But interestingly, parecon, by virtue of having balanced job complexes, makes remuneration conceptually trivial. We work at jobs with comparable quality of life implications and thus comparable overall sacrifice. Therefore we earn more or less only by virtue of working longer or working less long, or of working harder or working less hard. Decisions, as in every economic case, rest with the councils.

"Fourth, and certainly most complex, we need a new allocation system. The one that I advocate as part of parecon is called participatory planning. I reject markets because they promote anti-sociality, they reduce variety, they remunerate power or at best output (and of course property in capitalist variants), and they skew power to the ruling class (which is capitalists in one variant and the coordinator class in market socialism). I reject central planning also, because it is authoritarian and again skews power to the ruling coordinator class. Indeed, the central point is that we want classlessness but these existing allocation options, like the corporate division of labor that goes with them, produce class division and class rule. Thus arises the need for a different approach.

"Participatory planning uses a cooperative negotiation process to arrive at inputs and outputs for each workplace and at consumption items for each individual and also for each consumer council. Workers and consumers councils present their preferences. These are communicated and also summarized in diverse ways. Councils then make new proposals for inputs and outputs. This occurs through a number of rounds or iterations facilitated by various techniques and structures — mostly what are called facilitation boards. Relative valuations account for full social costs and benefits, transcending market incapacity to address goods with impact beyond the buyer and seller. Budgets are met, remuneration is equitable, outcomes are arrived at to directly pursue human wellbeing and development.

"But there is no center and periphery and there is no top and bottom. The incredible claim for participatory planning is not only that within workplace units there is self management, but that there also is self management for the economy as a whole."

I support the concept of a balanced job complex as a way of minimizing power imbalances yet this may also result in inefficiencies. It might make more sense for physically arduous or "rot" work to be concentrated amongst the young and physically capable. Also a major question mark of parecon is its allocation methods. I am not convinced that markets are all bad. Contrary to dominant ideology, markets predate capitalism. For instance, they existed — in an extensive form — in native communities of North America a thousand years ago. Parecon's market-less system appears overly focused on planning, which aside from possibly being inefficient can be both un-enjoyable and stifling of individual freedoms.

⦿ ⦿ ⦾ PRIMITIVISM — Another anarchist current that has some adherents around the world is primitivism. Primitivism.com (how ironic) explains primitivist philosophy: "Primitivism is the pursuit of ways of life running counter to the development of technology, its alienating antecedents, and the ensemble of changes wrought by both.

"Technology is here defined as tool use based upon division of labor...that is, tool manufacture and utilization that has become sufficiently complex to require specialization, implying both a separation and eventual stratification among individuals in the community, along with the rise of toil in the form of specialized, repetitive tasks."

Primitivism is, rightfully, a marginalized current within the anarchist milieu. While criticisms of technologies are abundant in left movements there is little evidence to suggest that

Syndicalists believe in the concept of the general strike as a revolutionary weapon

the answer for the many problems in the world is to return to the days of hunter-gathers. How would we feed the world's six plus billion people? Likewise, anthropological evidence suggests that while ancient societies were "anarchic" – no government – there were serious evils that most socialist libertarians would/should oppose.

⚫ ⚫ ⚫ SYNDICALISM — The central idea of syndicalism (which has had both anarchist and Marxist adherents) is that an alternative to capitalism can grow out of workers taking control of the economy through their industrial (as opposed to trade) unions. The work of syndicalists is to wrest control of industry from its capitalist owners and managers by organizing workplaces along radically democratic, non-hierarchical lines. In addition to class struggle, syndicalists usually support federalism, direct economic action, local autonomy and mutual aid. Syndicalists believe in the concept of the general strike as a revolutionary weapon.

The Industrial Workers of the World (IWW or Wobblies) at a recent anti-corporate globalization event distributed a flyer that exclaimed: "Globalize worker self-management, not corporate rule!" In a nutshell, this is the syndicalist answer to corporate globalization. The IWW, not always anarchist, has been influential within the syndicalist movement in North America. Their website explains that: "A struggle must go on until the workers of the world organize as a class, take possession of the means of production, abolish the wage system, and live in harmony with the Earth."

"We find that the centering of the management of industries into fewer and fewer hands makes the trade unions unable to cope with the ever growing power of the employing class. The trade unions foster a state of affairs which allows one set of workers to be pitted against another set of workers in the same industry, thereby helping defeat one another in wage wars. Moreover, the trade unions aid the employing class to mislead the workers into the belief that the working class have interests in common with their employers."

"These conditions can be changed and the interest of the working class upheld only by an organization formed in such a way that all its members in any one industry, or in all industries if necessary, cease work whenever a strike or lockout is on in any department thereof, thus making an injury to one an injury to all."

"Instead of the conservative motto, 'A fair day's wage for a fair day's work,' we must inscribe on our banner the revolutionary watchword, 'Abolition of the wage system.'

"It is the historic mission of the working class to do away with capitalism. The army of production must be organized, not only for everyday struggle with capitalists, but also to carry on production when capitalism shall have been overthrown. By organizing industrially we are forming the structure of the new society within the shell of the old."

While few seem to dislike Wobblies the way anarchists and Marxist-Leninists denounce each other, the high point of syndicalism seems to have been between 1905 and 1919. It has suffered because existing unions have mostly been quite antagonistic to its rank-and-file philosophy. It is likely a philosophy that would only come to the forefront in times of crisis, when existing, more bureaucratic union leadership is seen as hopeless, corrupt or irrelevant.

● ● ● DELEONISM — Another philosophy that has a long history, but a marginal effect is DeLeonism. Daniel DeLeon was editor of The People, from 1892 until his death in 1914 and founder of the Socialist Industrial Union program of the Socialist Labor Party in the USA. DeLeonism focuses on control over the economic realm. "The 'industrial form of government' which is to replace the political form would have only economic responsibilities." Thus DeLeon agreed with the anarchists, who believed that a truly classless society must also be stateless, and have no coercive power that is distinct from and ruling over the populace. "His philosophy differed from most anarchists and anarcho-syndicalists in his insistence that the working class can only abolish the state by first capturing control of it. The ballot, he said, 'raises the labor movement above the category of a conspiracy.'"

"However, the ballot is considered purely 'destructive', in that it seeks to attain control of the state only for the purpose of dismantling it. The sole 'constructive' power of the working class is considered to be the industrial union."

"The 'socialist industrial union' is conceived as an association of labor which organizes much as trade unions do, however it unites workers of all occupations as the integral departments of a single union of the entire working class. Furthermore, the union openly declares that, in putting forth momentary demands involving wages or working conditions, it is only biding its time. Once the degree of working class organization on both the political and industrial fields becomes sufficient, the union will 'take and hold' the means of production. At that point, the union will no longer be a means, but an end, its integral connection of all economic branches being put into place as the new system of management."

Again, while the philosophy sounds good, it has had little success in attracting adherents in the last hundred years.

⊛ ⊛ ⊛ ECONOMIC DEMOCRACY — A more recent trend that some might describe as syndicalist comes out of a broad non-Leninist Marxist tradition and calls for workers control and economic democracy. In his book A Manifesto of Economic Democracy Allan Engler (my uncle) explains how he conceptualizes a non-capitalist alternative:

"While worker-owned enterprises, producer and consumer cooperatives, and credit unions within capitalism are sometimes described as economic democracy, here it means replacing private capitalist title [ownership of companies] with social ownership and social entitlement. Economic democracy means replacing private dictatorships and master-servant relations [boss/employee] with workplace democracy.... Democracy and freedom in a world of social labor [the vast majority of work is accomplished socially] means social entitlement, social ownership, and workplace democracy. Social entitlement means the right of all to access means of livelihood, to employment, to capabilities, to opportunities, and to a fair share of social products. Social ownership means the right of everyone to a voice and vote in the direction of social means of livelihood. Workplace democracy means the right of everyone to participate in the democratic direction of their labor time. Self-employed individuals would direct their own labor time and exchange their products, but social means of livelihood would be socially owned and democratically directed... Social ownership—ownership by local, regional communities, nations, and perhaps international institutions—will be the structural foundation for social entitlement."

David Schweickart, in his book *Against Capitalism* argues that economic democracy would be a system where workers take over the existing economy and run it democratically. He is explicit in his defence of "the market" to allocate distribution of goods and services. While some might consider this capitalism without capitalists, Schweickart makes the case that such a system would retain the efficiencies of competition while ending the unequal distribution of power.

● ● ● THE POINT OF THIS CHAPTER has not been to steer anyone in a particular political direction, but rather to point out that all of us should do our own homework. Over the last two decades, since the fall of the Soviet Union and the pro-capitalist path taken by China, there has been no dominant alternative political vision to capitalism. Perhaps we have an opportunity for thousands of us around the world to discuss and refine a broad-based, non-sectarian, democratic political philosophy that can capture the hearts and minds of ordinary people.

CHAPTER SIXTEEN

HOW POLITICS IS SIMILAR TO HOCKEY

I don't know which feels better, scoring an overtime goal to win a big hockey game or writing a leaflet for a demonstration that draws ten thousand people. The experience of both is exhilarating. The commonality is a feeling of accomplishment. And politics, like hockey, is a team sport. Even if you don't make the big speech or score the winning goal, success is always the result of a collective effort. The feeling of accomplishment is all the better because it is shared with others.

One of the fundamental similarities between hockey and politics is that each individual must do the best they can with whatever skill level they possess, but the winning strategy is always playing for the team, not yourself. One hundred individuals playing as a team can beat many more individuals playing by themselves.

Activism, like hockey, should be fun. Being engaged feels good. Social bonds can be life-long. Demonstrations, like games, should be festive events. There is a sense of empowerment in knowing you are part of something much bigger than yourself. Taking everything too seriously is not a winning strategy. While politics, like junior hockey, can be a serious business you'll have more success if you enjoy a laugh now and then. If you don't take yourself too seriously, you'll be more fun to be around and so more people will want to be around you. The most important reason to be a political activist is to change the world into a better place. To me it seems obvious that the world will be a better place if more people have more fun more of the time.

Of course, success at hockey requires hard work. So too does politics. Just getting to know how the world works is a lifelong challenge. Reading, thinking and discussing are to politics like getting in shape is to hockey. You can't even get into the game if you are not in shape. Open your mind to the certainty that you don't know everything and that what exists might not be all that is possible.

One of the very best things you can do to improve your hockey skills is to play other sports. Table tennis improves fine motor reflexes. Playing football (real football, not American or Canadian) adds foot skills. Taking part in events outside politics makes you a more effective activist. Making connections through sports or music or theatre or volunteering allows those we need to reach to see us as ordinary people like them.

In politics, as in hockey, practice will get you as close to perfect as is humanly possible. The off-ice equivalent of skating, doing drills and scrimmaging is debating one-on-one, setting up tables and organizing meetings. You only learn how good you are by playing against others. You only know how good your ideas are by testing them in discussion with people who disagree. If you always scrimmage against the same opponents, you will never get better. Sectarian groups who only talk to each other will never blossom into large political currents. Often learning from a loss to a more powerful opponent is exactly what a team needs to improve. A successful season most often includes many defeats. If your desire is to make the world a better place by confronting authority, be prepared for many losing seasons before you get good enough to challenge for league supremacy.

Hockey can last a lifetime. While you can spend hours and hours trying to make it to the big leagues, in the end it may be more important to simply make the game a part of the way you stay in shape. There are professional players and recreational players with very different skill levels. One could argue that recreational playing is, in fact, more valuable to society. While there may be some "professional" activists and skill levels vary widely, there is absolutely no doubt that the most valuable player in politics is a collective award that can only go to millions of people around the world. The best players are those who integrate politics into their ordinary lives.

Skate, pass, get in position, shoot and score. Read, listen, analyze, discuss and act.